Russia Today and Conspiracy Theories

W0113685

The Russian international media outlet Russia Today (RT) has been widely accused in the Western world of producing government propaganda and conspiracy theories. This book explores for the first time the role that conspiracy theories actually play in the network's broadcasts.

More than this, it provides the first ever study of how the Russian government engages with conspiracy theories in the international arena, with a particular focus on the use of conspiracy theories as an instrument of public diplomacy. RT was established in 2005 to represent Russia to the world, and to present a Russian perspective on global events. Whilst some of RT's more overtly conspiratorial output has been taken off the air, the network remains a source of significant concern for governments and intelligence agencies in Europe and North America. Now, more than ever, policymakers, journalists, academics, and intelligence services alike seek to understand the role RT plays in the Russian government's foreign policy agenda. The authors use RT as a case study to investigate how global communication technologies influence the development and dissemination of conspiracy theories, which are also an important component of the post-Soviet Russian intellectual landscape and Kremlin-sponsored political discourse.

This book will appeal to students and scholars of Politics and International Relations, Russian Studies, and Conspiracy Theories.

Ilya Yablokov is a Lecturer in Journalism and Media at the University of Sheffield, UK. His areas of expertise are Russian media and international broadcasting, Russian politics, conspiracy theories, mis- and disinformation campaigns as well as problems of censorship and self-censorship in today's media.

Precious N Chatterje-Doody is a Lecturer in Politics and International Studies at the Open University, UK. Her areas of expertise are Russian foreign and security policy, soft power, information politics, and political communication.

Conspiracy Theories

Series Editors: Peter Knight, *University of Manchester,* and Michael Butter, *University of Tübingen.*

Conspiracy theories have a long history and exist in all modern societies. However, their visibility and significance are increasing today. Conspiracy theories can no longer be simply dismissed as the product of a pathological mind-set located on the political margins. This series provides a nuanced and scholarly approach to this most contentious of subjects. It draws on a range of disciplinary perspectives including political science, sociology, history, media and cultural studies, area studies and behavioural sciences. Issues covered include the psychology of conspiracy theories, changes in conspiratorial thinking over time, the role of the Internet, regional and political variations and the social and political impact of conspiracy theories.

The series will include edited collections, single-authored monographs and short-form books.

Europe: Continent of Conspiracies
Conspiracy Theories in and about Europe
Edited by Andreas Önnerfors and André Krouwel

Russia Today and Conspiracy Theories
People, Power and Politics on RT
Ilya Yablokov and Precious N Chatterje-Doody

Conspiracy Theories and Latin American History
Lurking in the Shadows
Luis Roniger and Leonardo Senkman

For more information about this series, please visit: https://www.routledge.com/Routledge-Studies-in-Genocide-and-Crimes-against-Humanity/book-series/RSGCH

Russia Today and Conspiracy Theories

People, Power and Politics on RT

**Ilya Yablokov and
Precious N Chatterje-Doody**

Routledge
Taylor & Francis Group

LONDON AND NEW YORK

First published 2022
by Routledge
2 Park Square, Milton Park, Abingdon, Oxon OX14 4RN

and by Routledge
605 Third Avenue, New York, NY 10158

Routledge is an imprint of the Taylor & Francis Group, an informa business

© 2022 Ilya Yablokov and Precious N Chatterje-Doody

British Library Cataloguing-in-Publication Data
A catalogue record for this book is available from the British Library

Library of Congress Cataloging-in-Publication Data
Names: Yablokov, Ilya, author. | Chatterje-Doody,
Precious N, author.
Title: Russia Today and conspiracy theories : people,
power and politics on RT / Ilya Yablokov and
Precious N Chatterje-Doody.
Description: Abingdon, Oxon ; New York : Routledge, 2021. |
Series: Conspiracy theories | Includes bibliographical
references and index.
Identifiers: LCCN 2021011203 (print) | LCCN 2021011204
(ebook) | ISBN 9780367224677 (hardback) | ISBN
9780367697013 (paperback) | ISBN 9780367224684 (ebook)
Subjects: LCSH: RT (Television network) | Television
broadcasting of news. | Mass media and propaganda—Russia
(Federation) | Conspiracy theories—Russia (Federation) |
Russia (Federation)—Foreign relations—Western countries. |
Russia (Federation)—Politics and government—1991–
Classification: LCC PN4888.T4 Y33 2021 (print) |
LCC PN4888.T4 (ebook) | DDC 070.195—dc23
LC record available at https://lccn.loc.gov/2021011203
LC ebook record available at https://lccn.loc.gov/2021011204

ISBN: 978-0-367-22467-7 (hbk)
ISBN: 978-0-367-69701-3 (pbk)
ISBN: 978-0-367-22468-4 (ebk)

Typeset in Times New Roman
by codeMantra

Contents

Acknowledgements   vii

Introduction: the curious case of RT   1

1 Conspiracy theories, the evolution of
   communication and the contemporary global
   media environment   6

2 'Question more'? The Kremlin's strategy behind RT   19

3 The world according to the Truthseekers   33

4 Conspiracy and democracy: election meddling
   and #TrumpRussia   53

5 Conspiracy and crisis: narrative holes and
   the Skripal affair   69

6 RT in the post-pandemic world   85

   Conclusion   101

   Index   107

Acknowledgements

First and foremost, we would like to express our gratitude to Profs. Peter Knight and Michael Butter, primary investigators of the EU COST initiative 'Comparative analysis of conspiracy theories' for their support in publishing this book. Thanks to their tireless work in the academic study of conspiracy theories and their agreement with Routledge we have had a chance to share our latest explorations of these most topical issues. We would also like to thank Profs. Vera Tolz and Stephen Hutchings at the University of Manchester who have been so generous with their expertise, enthusiasm and encouragement, and given us the opportunity to learn from the best in the field.

We are indebted to our families and loved ones for their support and tolerance in seeing us exploring some of the most bizarre topics on a daily basis.

Introduction
The curious case of RT

On 5 July 1881 the unknown author of an editorial in the *St. Louis Daily Globe* – a Democrat newspaper in one of the Midwest American states, published a piece about the assassination of the 20th US President James Garfield. According to historian Andrew McKenzie-McHarg, this journalist was the first to use the term 'conspiracy theory' to reflect upon the myriad of versions of Garfield's murder that emerged (McKenzie-McHarg, 2017, p. 75). Since then – and especially since the German sociologist Karl Popper used the term in the late 1940s (Butter, 2020), the phenomenon of conspiracy theories has occupied a totally different space in our lives, reflecting how many humans interpret reality. In fact, reality becomes more mind-blowing than the starkest conspiratorial fiction. The 1999 film *The Matrix* depicted the world as an illusion fed to humans whose bodies are used as batteries powering the *Matrix* – an enormous computer run by AI – that keeps the majority of people unable to perceive reality as it is. This postmodernist criticism of capitalism is perceived differently in 2020 when AI algorithms underlie the multibillion businesses of big tech, shaping 'the surveillance capitalism' (Zuboff, 2019) in which we all live. The conspiracy of computers against humans doesn't look as unrealistic as it once was.

Scholars have recognised that uncertainty and insecurity about the true nature of the world lie behind belief in conspiracies (Harambam and Aupers, 2017). As Frederic Jameson (1988) argued, conspiracy theories are 'a poor person's cognitive mapping in the postmodern age'. Knight and Butter suggest (2020) that Jameson's perception of conspiracy theories treats the emergence of conspiracy theories not as a product of a mentally sick mind, but as an allegory of the overly complicated world. This approach helps identify conspiracy theories as a symbol of disbalance of power and influence in society. Often conveyed through populist politics, that divide of the social between the people and the power – a characteristic of conspiracy theories – explains why these ideas have such huge power in politics today (Fenster, 2008).

People, power and *politics* are the key to understanding the proliferation of conspiracy theories in the modern world via the media and, as it stands, the three terms that appear in the subtitle of this book. We come to a focus on these elements of contemporary international broadcasting to explore how conspiracy theories are communicated globally via the means of traditional and new media by (a) claiming to represent 'the people', (b) undermining and relocating power between political actors and thus, (c) shaping sub-national, national and global politics.

One may ask: why RT? What made us write a book on the seemingly obscure media outlet whose viewing numbers are almost impossible to figure out, but which has gleefully repeated politicians' accusations that it is a 'propaganda bullhorn' in its own advertising (RT, 2014)? Well, because RT presents a curious case of an international media organisation that has instrumentalised conspiracy theories and turned them into a tool of international politics. And given the rapidity of global communications and how quickly societies are divided in terms of profits and opinions, it is clear that RT is not the only media that does, or will continue, to benefit from these divides.

RT was established in 2005 (as Russia Today) to represent Russia to the world and to present a Russian perspective on global events. Very quickly, the network began actively producing and promoting conspiracy theories. Whilst some of RT's more overtly conspiratorial output has since been taken off the air, the network remains a source of significant concern for governments and intelligence agencies, who have feared its potential to influence public opinion during recent elections, referenda and hostile state interventions. Now, more than ever, policymakers, journalists, academics and intelligence services alike seek to understand how RT helps to turn obscure ideas and social doubts into tools of international politics.

This book draws on the fields of International Relations, Politics and Media Studies, and sets conspiracy theories within this context as a populist instrument of power relations (Fenster, 2008). In today's rapidly globalising world, international broadcasting and public diplomacy more broadly, are seen as vital sources of potential influence on overseas audiences. RT represents an excellent case for the investigation of how global communication technologies influence the development and dissemination of conspiracy theories, which are also an important component of the post-Soviet Russian intellectual landscape and Kremlin sponsored political discourse (Yablokov, 2018).

In uniting these two research areas, this book explores how RT's engagement with conspiracy theory allows it to articulate a critique of the policies of the US and Western European governments as if from *within* those societies. Far from delivering the external critiques of a foreign power, RT performs as a vessel for aggrieved parties within its audiences, who are actively involved in packaging conspiracy theories. RT's strategic use of new media feeds into this process by enabling targeting of outputs to specific audience contingents, thus transforming international broadcasting into a phenomenon of peculiar domestic relevance. With this foregrounding and engagement with different types of conspiracy theories which have currency amongst the general public as an interpretative frame of reality, RT's outputs conform to what Peter Knight defines as a 'conspiracy culture'. This allows RT to infuse the current social and economic inequalities of Western society with conspiratorial allegations, thereby addressing international audiences with a distinctly anti-elitist message (Knight, 2000).

According to RT, global media heavyweights (like CNN) are in league with the political establishment. So, RT's development has to be situated in relation to both the abundant tradition of populism in the US, and the rise in populist movements and trends across the globe. With its slogan encouraging audiences to 'Question more', RT brands itself as a direct challenge to these elites and their visions of current affairs. Its expansion of broadcast and online service provision to cover media markets across Western Europe, Latin America and the Arabic speaking world demonstrates sustained Russian interest in influencing and interacting with public opinion across a range of global societies. For this reason, it is crucial to explore the ways in which RT's programming incorporates, and responds to, the perspectives of anti-establishment right-wing and left-wing communities in the societies where it targets its outputs. To do this comprehensively, we have focussed our analysis on the English language outputs of RT and their circulation within the international Anglophone media space. We don't engage here with the stories that have been broadcast in French, German, Spanish or Arabic, nor how these distinct language services have interacted in their own respective sections of the international media.

This interactivity is crucial to understanding how the expression of populist sentiment adopts new forms in the digital era, as core and peripheral audiences across multiple platforms co-produce, re-write and disseminate these ideas. Thus, media actors as varied as RT, the platforms upon which it makes its outputs available, its media contributors and audiences all contribute to producing the emotional arguments that stimulate engagement, to influence wider transnational discussion and enable today's conspiracy myths to flourish. The book interrogates these processes of production, evolution and dissemination of conspiratorial ideas on and around RT. This means not only tracing the origins of some conspiratorial ideas in the political culture of America or particular Western European states, but also investigating the more dynamic processes of how RT's outputs interact with global conspiracy cultures and trigger further conspiracy myth making amongst both sub-national and transnational communities. Presenting evidence from a series of recent case studies, the book investigates the political implications of conspiracy theories on and around RT – ranging from the network's overt engagement with conspiracy theories as a genre, through to their more subtle integration into the reporting of newsworthy events.

Structure of the book

The first chapter provides a short overview of how the form and dissemination of conspiracy theories have been historically intertwined with the evolution of communication technologies, before taking a deep dive into the contemporary media environment, and the ways in which this facilitates the spread of conspiracy theories. Chapter 2 outlines the network's history, explaining the Kremlin's motivations behind its creation, and the reasons that RT developed into a media outlet focussed specifically on the spread of conspiracy theories. The subsequent chapters explore the editorial strategies chosen by RT's staff, and their intertwinement with conspiratorial narratives. In Chapter 3, we investigate two programmes – *The Truthseeker* and *The World According to Jesse Ventura* – which serve as examples of how RT has instrumentalised conspiracy theories from both far right- and left-wing ideologies, providing both with an arena for expressing dissatisfaction. Chapters 4 and 5 deal with stories of immense international political significance to Russia's political leadership, and in which RT has played an important mediating role. First, Donald Trump's unexpected victory in the 2016 presidential elections, and second, the 2018 poisoning of former Russian-British double agent, Sergei Skripal and his daughter in the British city of Salisbury. Together these events fed into the Kremlin's reputation as a global 'bad guy' prepared to hack foreign governments and poison civilians to sew chaos and panic. RT's reporting, however, adopted conspiracy theories to report them in terms of Western governments' anti-Russian provocations. Our final chapter, number 6, investigates RT's outputs over the pandemic period – bringing to light how inter-related conspiracy theories have permeated coverage of both COVID-19 and the highly contentious 2020 US Presidential election campaign. Written as the impact of these massive social and political ruptures continues to be felt across the globe, the conclusion of the book reflects on the curious place of RT within the broader context of contemporary conspiracy cultures that are unlikely to disappear any time soon. It offers a range of recommendations for addressing how the perennial politics of conspiracy theories permeates our contemporary age.

References

Butter, M. (2020). *The Nature of Conspiracy Theories*. Cambridge: Polity.

Fenster, M. (2008). *Conspiracy Theories: Secrecy and Power in American Culture*. Minneapolis: University of Minnesota Press.

Harambam J. and Aupers, S. (2017). "I Am Not a Conspiracy Theorist': Relational Identifications in the Dutch Conspiracy Milieu'. *Cultural Sociology*, 11(1), pp. 113–129.

Jameson, F. (1988). 'Cognitive Mapping', in C. Nelson and L. Grossberg (eds.) *Marxism and the Interpretation of Culture*. Basingstoke: Macmillan, pp. 347–358.

Knight, P. (2000). *Conspiracy Culture: From Kennedy to the X-Files*. London: Routledge.

Knight, P. and Butter, M. (2020). 'Conspiracy theories in historical, cultural and literary studies,' in P. Knight and M. Butter (eds.) *Routledge Handbook of Conspiracy Theories*. London: Routledge, pp. 28–42.

McKenzie-McHarg, A. (2017). 'Conspiracy Theory: The Nineteenth-Century Prehistory of a Twentieth-Century Concept', in J. Uscinski (ed.) *Conspiracy Theories and the People Who Believe It*. New York: Oxford University Press, pp. 63–78.

RT (2014). "Propaganda Bullhorn': John Kerry Attacks RT during Ukraine Address', RT, 25 April [Online]. Available at: https://www.rt.com/news/154760-kerry-attacks-rt-propaganda/ (Accessed: 17 November 2020).

Yablokov, I. (2018). *Fortress Russia: Conspiracy Theories in the Post-Soviet World*. Cambridge: Polity.

Zuboff, S. (2019). *The Age of Surveillance Capitalism: The Fight for a Human Future at the New Frontier of Power*. New York: Public Affairs.

1 Conspiracy theories, the evolution of communication and the contemporary global media environment

Conspiracy theories are a recurrent feature of politics, and have evolved over centuries alongside developments in communication and political rhetoric. In Ancient Athens, conspiracy accusations were used to control society, by reminding citizens of the need to be accountable to the republic (Roisman, 2006). In Ancient Rome, conspiracy rhetoric was used both to destroy opponents' reputations and to help explain political events that were otherwise hard to account for rationally (Pagan, 2012). Crucially, in both societies, there was some capacity for political leaders to be challenged by their opponents for their actions, and conspiracy theories worked as a political tool to help manage public politics. In the late Middle Ages conspiracy theories re-emerged as a by-product of early European political developments, such as how Italian establishment powerbrokers analysed information from numerous – often anonymous – sources to make decisions about the security of their states (Zwierlein and de Graaf, 2013). Later, this style of thinking spread across the European societies that were gradually becoming divided along religious lines. The key to the proliferation of conspiracy theories in modern Europe, then, for the first time since Antiquity, was the amount of news communication produced and received across the European continent (Zwierlein, 2020, p. 546). Making sense of the political sphere became important to princes, office holders and intellectuals alike, whilst the threat of censorship increased the anonymity of this communication.

The Age of Enlightenment turned conspiracy theories into a major cognitive instrument to comprehend the rapidly changing reality. In just a couple of years, networks of intellectuals in Britain, Europe, Russia and the US were vital in spreading the first global conspiracy theory about an 'Illuminati' secret society (Porter, 2005). From the onset of the American republic, populist movements instrumentalised anti-Illuminati and later anti-immigrant fears, turning conspiracy theories into tools of social mobilisation (Davis, 1960; Hofstadter, 1965). In Europe, conservatives quickly merged anti-Illuminati and anti-Semitic conspiracy theories, as with the late 19th-century 'letter of Simonini' hoax, which claimed that the Jews stood behind the Masonic lodges and were responsible for the waves of European revolutions (Oberhauser, 2020). Jews became seen as a problematic 'Other' whose place amongst the newly forming nations was unstable and even threatening (Bartal, 2005).

Shortly afterwards, Russian counterintelligence officers produced a faked document, *The Protocols of the Elders of Zion* (Hagemeister, 2008). Its premise was that of a secret meeting of Jewish elders from around the world, scheming to achieve future political and financial omnipotence. The scale and velocity with which this hoax spread globally in the first decades of the 20th century – and its enduring relevance today – reveal much about the frustrations shared in Russia, Germany and America about rapidly changing life, and the appetite for scapegoats. Both the narrative and the visual elements of *The Protocols* helped channel hatred towards real Jewish communities (Gray, 2010) and even imagined ones (Swami, 2012).

Marshall McLuhan's famous concept 'the medium is the message' (1964) explains how the evolution of the media in their relation to human senses has impacted upon conspiratorial narratives and their means of circulation in the last couple of centuries (Aupers et al., 2020). Where printed stories have helped to make conspiracy a popular way of explaining reality, visual representations of conspiracy have captivated mass audiences, especially during political and financial crises. Anti-Semitic tropes developed from late 19th-century Nazi propaganda featuring the eternal Jew, to 20th-century conspiratorial cartoons and film, all the way up to early 21st-century memes and GIFs. On the other hand, the Cold War offered an opportunity for the conspiracy cultures that had flourished for centuries in the US (Goldberg, 2001), Europe (Onnerfors and Krouwel, 2021) and Russia (Yablokov, 2018) to come to the fore as a transnational political tool. In fact, there are few differences between the nature of Stalinist propaganda against capitalists and the McCarthyite Red-baiting of the 1950s. However, the espionage-focussed mentality of the Cold War turned conspiracy theories into a legitimate style of cultural and political story-telling (Thalmann, 2019) that continues to permeate the politics of the US and Russia to this day (Denvir, 2018; Yablokov, 2018). Clearly, the visual and narrative culture of conspiracy theories can adapt to fit the prevailing media context (Caumanns and Onnerfors, 2020). In this respect, the current period is particularly significant, because of individuals' ability to 'prosume' (Ritzer and Jurgenson, 2010): to consume and produce their very own conspiratorial readings of the balance of power underlying world events (Aupers, 2012).

Conspiracy theories and the logics of the contemporary global media environment

Conspiracy theories spread rapidly in a contemporary global media environment in which over half of the global population uses the internet, and in developed countries, regular use is the norm (85% of EU adults; 91% of UK adults) (ITU, 2018; ONS, 2018). News and information can now be 'prosumed' instantaneously, right when trust in established institutions is seeing a long-term fall and people are more open to trusting alternative figureheads who better reflect their own personal perspectives (Coleman, 2018, p. 1). All media institutions have had to adapt to this context, with many attempting to maximise and monetise online consumption through 'clickbait' (Moore, 2018; Chatterje-Doody and Crilley, 2019a). Such trends also help to explain how marginal actors and discourse can come to influence the agendas of others – especially given that conservative news websites are more likely than liberal ones to propagate fabricated stories, and conservative individuals are more likely to believe them. Liberal media outlets, on the other hand, are the ones more likely to change their agenda in response (Vargo et al., 2018).

At the same time, the increased personalisation of news allows media users to actively curate and contribute to the information they consume. Production, dissemination and reception of news are now intimately intertwined (Chadwick, 2017), and users contribute to feedback loops that shape the media-politics relationship (Zannettou et al., 2017). Just as social media users are more trusting of the opinions and recommendations of their contacts (Turcotte et al., 2015; Rosenthal and Brito, 2017, p. 382), so too mainstream news coverage cites social media commentary and trends as examples of public opinion (Chatterje-Doody and Crilley, 2019a, p. 84). This gives online minorities the opportunity to influence offline news agendas.

With established systems of generating knowledge and trust in crisis, many people doubt that political elites and the mainstream media represent their true interests. The current media environment increases their access to alternative interpretations of current events that ring more true to them (Davies, 2018). So, truth becomes de-linked from analysis of public records, debate and consensus-building. Instead, credibility attaches itself to the 'new type of heroic truth teller' who is 'brave enough to call bullshit on the rest of the establishment' (Davies, 2018).

Various political and media actors have positioned themselves as precisely such heroic truth tellers, often whilst explicitly criticising the 'establishment'. They include whistle-blowers like Edward Snowden, independent publishers like WikiLeaks, alternative news outlets (whether domestic or international) that promote these kinds of stories, and individuals who build their profile by commenting on them. This division of the public space into a noble people set against a corrupt elite is a classic feature of populist logic. These populist logics of communication work with the dynamics of the contemporary global media environment in ways that define conspiracy theories in the present age.

The linked logics of populism and conspiracy theories

Populism has been referred to as a 'thin-centred ideology' that political actors can map onto any specific ideological concerns they have, from either end of the political spectrum (Mudde and Kaltwasser, 2017). In practical terms, though, populism often involves exploiting particular issue politics at times of real or perceived crisis and societal dissatisfaction (Canovan, 1999). For this reason, several scholars look at populism in terms of what it actually *does* – i.e. as 'a political logic' (Laclau, 2005), a 'style' of performing and thus enacting social relations (Moffit and Tormey, 2014) or, most recently, as a 'communication logic' which incorporates an actor's claims, motives and methods of engagement (Engesser et al., 2017).

Broadly speaking, populist appeals tend to mobilise 'the people' against power-holding 'elites' who are depicted as corrupt, self-serving and out of touch with 'ordinary' citizens' problems (Taggart, 2000; Davies, 2018, p. 220). Dominant cultural norms and styles – like formal dress and language choices – are often rejected in preference to 'non-elite' forms, such as MAGA baseball caps, colloquialisms or obscene language (Canovan, 2004, p. 242; Moffitt and Tormey, 2014, p. 389; Mudde and Kaltwasser, 2017, p. 10). Conspiracy theories are structured precisely around this crucial opposition between 'the people' and a scheming 'elite'. They represent a populist interpretation of how power works: powerful elites serve their own interests at the expense of the public (Fenster, 2008; Yablokov, 2018). Indeed, studies have shown that openness to the populist values of people-centrism and anti-elitism is associated with openness to conspiracy theories (Castanho Silva et al., 2017). What is more, belief in any conspiracy theory increases openness to others, regardless of whether they fit coherently together (Goertzel, 1994; Wood et al., 2012).

Today's rapid, accessible media environment offers people a veritable buffet of populist ideas and conspiracy theories for interpreting reality: the interaction between different media, host platforms and market logics means that journalists frequently produce content intended to appeal to the assumed preferences of intended (nonelite) audiences. Often this takes on populist characteristics, particularly in the most commercially motivated media products, and those closely based upon the vox populi (Mazzoleni et al., 2003; Bos and Brants, 2014). This is particularly notable with online media, where assumptions about preferences are not necessary – outputs can be geared towards the kind of content that audiences actually engage with. As it happens, online audiences are more likely to share and believe fake news of a conspiratorial bent (Silverman, 2016; Silverman and Singer-Vine, 2016). What is more, conspiracy beliefs increase where news media environments foreground stories about conspiracies (Udani et al., 2018; Weeks, 2018). With the contemporary media environment defined by circulation between social and other online media (Engesser et al., 2017, p. 1280), this means that populist and conspiratorial messaging often ends up being produced through the various interactions between global media, the journalists who produce it, the platforms it is produced and circulated on, and the audiences that interact with it. This cycle gives conspiratorial online content a market advantage, and it is often packaged to engage audiences' emotions, rather than just their reason (Chatterje-Doody and Crilley, 2019b).

In fact, people's understandings of the world do not rely on reason alone. Emotions shape 'the taken-for-granted assumptions' (Fierke, 2013, p. 209), that structure people's thought processes, and this helps explain why conspiracy theories tend to 'appeal to individuals who seek accuracy and/or meaning, but perhaps lack the cognitive tools or experience problems that prevent them from being able to find accuracy and meaning via other more rational means' (Douglas et al, 2019, p. 8). For those individuals seeking to find news commentary that more closely matches their own perception of the world, the increasingly crowded global media marketplace offers a wealth of alternative sources on which they can draw, and which instinctively feel as though they offer a more compelling explanation of current events.

Together with the ubiquity of access to social media platforms, this makes the spread of conspiracy theories much easier. As the 2016 viral 'Pizzagate' conspiracy theory shows, it might take less than three months from someone alleging on Facebook that the leaders of the US Democratic Party are a part of a paedophile sex ring, to real-world violence breaking out in response (Robb, 2017). Similarly, the rapid spread of QAnon conspiracy theories about Donald Trump's fight against a cabal of Democrats and celebrities (LaFrance, 2020) saw major social networks ban QAnon communities over fears that their misinformation and conspiracy theories could affect the outcome of the 2020 US presidential elections (Wong, 2020); their links to the physical breach of the US Capitol building in early 2021 is the subject of ongoing criminal investigation at the time of writing.

This, in short, explains not only the recurring draw of conspiracy theories over time, but also the ways in which their circulation and political implications are intimately intertwined with the prevailing communications environment. The unprecedented rapidity and interconnectivity of the current global marketplace of ideas and trends in which media organisations such as RT operate shapes the ways in which they make their appeals, and feeds into the social and political impact of conspiracy theories today.

Alternative news, conspiracy confirmation bias and RT's brand identity

Technological changes since at least the 1990s have vastly altered the media landscape. Broadcasting (even by public service broadcasters) has become increasingly consumer-focussed (Blummler and Kavanagh, 1999, p. 220) – a trend only exacerbated by the switch online (Moore, 2018). More partisan outlets also emerged to meet consumer demand. For example, Fox News in the US was created to 'appeal directly to the conservative Everyman' with figures from Republican politics brought on board right from the start (Sommerlad, 2018). The same period saw many states create or expand their international broadcasting operations in order to communicate via television with the general public in other countries.[1] European networks including the BBC and Deutsche Welle (now DW) were generally building on longstanding radio operations. Important overseas promotional tools during the periods of Empire and the Cold War, they often emphasise their educational merit, as in the DW slogan: 'made for minds'. Newer networks founded from outside Europe, however, have presented themselves as challengers to the dominant perspectives of such Western media institutions. Thus, Al Jazeera seeks to provide a 'voice for the voiceless'; TRT World encourages global audiences to 'see world events differently' and RT, as we shall see further, invites its audiences to 'Question More' – not just about global politics itself, but, crucially, about how the mainstream media represents such politics.[2]

Over the same period, mass access to the internet and the low costs of publishing online enabled the rise of new media players. These included special interest news and current affairs roundups, which have since evolved into influential news organisations (e.g. Drudge Report (1995), HuffPost (2005), Breitbart (2007)). This choice-focussed environment has dented the circulation figures for many established news providers (Barthel, 2017), prompting various initiatives to make content more accessible and audience-focussed (Blummler and Kavanagh, 1999, p. 220; Chatterje-Doody and Crilley, 2019a, p. 84). For other news providers, it has opened up opportunities: it simplifies the production of low-quality filler content ('churnalism'), like social media trend reporting (Ramsay and Robertshaw, 2018); it provides cheap, global dissemination for many of the new international broadcasters (al-Nashmi et al., 2017); it has facilitated citizen-journalism via social media and blog platforms (Allan, 2013) and crucially, it enables digitally empowered citizens to discuss the news in real time.

Each of these differing news types has contrasting claims to legitimacy, making the rapid dissemination of falsehoods, or 'fake news' very easy. A range of initiatives has emerged to combat 'fake news', including fact-checking software (Booth, 2017), and major media organisations' own fact-checking and picture/video verification initiatives. The concerns have also prompted engagement from regulators and social networks, as demonstrated by Facebook's third-party fact-checking partnerships; changes to YouTube's recommender algorithm (since 2019) and Twitter's practice of flagging false claims around the 2020 US Presidential election. Journalist-led 'slow news' movements have also arisen to promote an alternative model in practice (e.g. Tortoise media).

The Russian state has frequently been accused of harnessing this environment to undermine the institutions and practices of democracy in the West (Jamieson, 2019). The combination of high consumer choice, variable public trust and a crowded media marketplace increase the importance of audiences' feelings in determining the sources that they consider reliable. This is key to understanding RT and its relationship with conspiracy culture. Initially founded as Russia Today in 2005, RT forms an important pillar of the Russian state's strategy for communicating with foreign audiences. Yet, the network is also in many ways a product of the contemporary media environment, and has developed in ways that suit this context particularly well.

First, RT's mission and brand identity are a perfect fit with the current media environment. Similarly to the other newer international broadcasters, RT expressly presents itself as an alternative to a Western-dominated mainstream media establishment. Its Russian perspective on world affairs supposedly equips audiences to 'Question More' about the news. The selling point of this perspective, then, is not that it is Russian, but that it has outsider status. This is central to understanding how RT markets itself and its brand ethos within an environment of declining public trust in established institutions: RT positions itself as precisely the 'heroic truth-teller' that can call bullshit on Western political and mainstream media establishments (Davies, 2018). Indeed, the network's successive advertising campaigns have foregrounded this status. For instance, one recent promotional video sees a variety of RT contributors re-claim the 'useful idiot' label that had been levelled at them as evidence that they had fearlessly spoken truth to corrupt power (RT, 2017). Tellingly, the opening frame of this video highlights that the label had initially been conferred on RT contributors by 'an NGO sponsored by Soros'. The observation appears intended simultaneously to discredit the organisation (and its claims) as partisan, as well as to bring to mind the raft of conspiracy theories that circulate online about the billionaire financier, without needing to make explicit allegations (Buzzfeed, 2020). RT's brand identity is therefore built on its capacity to raise questions, rather than having to provide any detail or credible answers. This is a practice that RT has developed over time, in which it makes conspiratorial insinuations rather than outright allegations. Similar logics are applied when engaging with the topic of 'fake news'. Just as the investment of George Soros in developing fact-checking software (Booth, 2017) offers space for conspiracy theories to claim that fact-checking is a scam by the 'elite', so RT calls into doubt similar initiatives and their motives. The network has launched its own fact-checking page, whose focus is to debunk what it presents as false claims about RT itself.[3]

RT's questioning of conventional wisdom is further reflected in its preferred topics and analysts. Many RT commentators are regulars either on the network itself, or on its sister radio outlet, Sputnik. A significant proportion formerly held positions in establishment institutions, but left as whistle-blowers. Of those commentators remaining close to political power, the three main groups tend to be representatives of the Russian political elite, or of European fringe left- and right-wing parties. Various other commentators represent NGOs and interest groups that document establishment breaches. So, even without needing to intervene editorially in what guests choose to articulate, RT overwhelmingly represents perspectives from the margins. This focus on questioning mainstream and 'establishment' accounts creates a strong coherence with conspiracy culture, that need not necessarily make sense overall. In this way, RT benefits from not having to maintain audience trust in its impartiality and balance, in the way that more established broadcasters like the BBC have to (something which is becoming increasingly challenging). Rather, RT's appeal need only be rather more partial: it draws attention to things that do not feel quite right, or that don't add up. Its marketing relies on audiences being able to accept that something undetermined is missing in the dominant explanations of world news, and RT's willingness to note this is a key element of its brand credibility. This credibility, however, does not demand the ability to offer an alternative coherent explanation. It is likely that this feature of RT's output makes it particularly attractive to people with a pre-existing openness to conspiracy theories, since research has already shown that '[p]eople who overestimate their ability to understand complex causal phenomena are also prone to conspiracy beliefs' (cited in Douglas et al., 2019, p. 7). What is more, the network has honed its relationship with conspiracy culture over time, in ways that consistently take advantage of the features of an evolving media environment. As the following chapter makes clear, RT's evolution over time reflects a series of priorities and logics that have long occupied the attention of Russia's current ruling elite.

Notes

1 UK's BBC World (1991); Germany's DW (1992); EuroNews (1993); China's CGTN (2000); Russia's RT (then Russia Today) and Venezuela's Telesur (2005); France's France24 and Qatar's Al Jazeera (2006); Iran's PressTV (2007); Turkey's TRTWorld (2015).
2 See the networks' respective 'about' statements at https://www.aljazeera.com/aboutus/; https://www.trtworld.com/about and https://www.rt.com/about-us/
3 For more detail, see https://www.rt.com/facts-vs-fiction/

References

al Nashmi, E., North, M., Bloom, T. and Cleary, J. (2017). 'Promoting a Global Brand: A Study of International News Organisations' YouTube Channels', *The Journal of International Communication*, 23(2), pp. 165–185.

Allan, S. (2013). *Citizen Witnessing: Revisioning Journalism in Times of Crisis*, 1st ed. Cambridge: Polity.

Aupers, S. (2012). '"Trust no one": Modernization, paranoia and conspiracy culture', *European Journal of Communication*, 27(1), pp. 22–34.

Aupers S., Craciun D., Onnerfors A. (2020). 'Introduction' in Knight P. and M. Butter (eds.) *Routledge Handbook of Conspiracy Theories*. London: Routledge, pp. 387–390.

Bartal, I. (2005). *The Jews of Eastern Europe, 1772–1881.* Philadelphia: University of Pennsylvania Press.

Barthel, M. (2017). 'Despite Subscription Surges for Largest U.S. Newspapers, Circulation and Revenue Fall for Industry Overall', *Pew Research Center*, 1 June [Online]. Available at: http://www.pewresearch.org/facttank/2017/06/01/circulation-and-revenuefall-for-newspaper-industry/ (Accessed: 12 November 2020).

Booth, R. (2017). 'Journalists to Use 'Immune System' Software against Fake News', *The Guardian*, 8 August [Online]. Available at: https://www.theguardian.com/technology/2017/aug/08/fake-news-full-fact-software-immune-system-journalism-soros-omidyar (Accessed: 26 February 2020).

Bos, L. and Brants, K. (2014). 'Populist Rhetoric in Politics and Media: A Longitudinal Study of the Netherlands', *European Journal of Communication*, 29(6), pp. 703–719.

Buzzfeed. (2020). 'Listen: The Reality Behind The George Soros Conspiracy Theories', *Buzzfeed*, 9 July [Online]. Available at: https://www.buzzfeed.com/newsoclock/truth-behind-george-soros-conspiracy-theories-podcast (Accessed: 11 November 2020).

Canovan, M. (2004). 'Populism for Political Theorists?', *Journal of Political Ideologies*, 9(3), pp. 241–252.

Castanho Silva, B., Vegetti, F. and Littvay, L. (2017). 'The Elite Is Up to Something: Exploring the Relation between Populism and Belief in Conspiracy Theories', *Swiss Political Science Review*, 23(4), pp. 423–443.

Caumanns U. and Onnerfors A. (2020). 'Conspiracy theories and visual culture', in Knight P., and Butter M. (eds.) *Routledge Handbook of Conspiracy Theories.* London: Routledge, pp. 441–456.

Chatterje-Doody, P.N. and Crilley, R. (2019a). 'Populism and Contemporary Global Media: Populist Communication Logics and the Co-construction of Transnational Identities', in Stengel, F.A., MacDonald, D.B. and Nabers, D. (eds.) *Populism and World Politics: Exploring Inter- and Transnational Dimensions.* London: Palgrave Macmillan, pp. 73–99.

Chatterje-Doody, P.N. and Crilley, R. (2019b). 'Making Sense of Emotions and Affective Investments in War: RT and the Syrian Conflict on YouTube', *Media and Communication*, 7(3), pp. 167–178.

Coleman, S. (2018). 'Introduction', *European Journal of Communication*, 33(2), pp. 117–121.

Davis, D.B. (1960). 'Some Themes of Counter-Subversion: An Analysis of Anti-Masonic, Anti-Catholic, and Anti-Mormon Literature', *The Mississippi Valley Historical Review* 47(2), pp. 205–224.

Davies, W. (2018). *Nervous States: How Feeling Took over the World.* London: Jonathan Cape.

Denvir D. (2018). 'The Psychology of Russiagate'. *Jacobin Mag.* Available at: https://www.jacobinmag.com/2018/04/russiagate-surveillance-politics-russian-trolls-greenwald (Accessed: 11 November 2020).

Douglas, K., Uscinski J.E., Sutton, R.M., Cichocka, A., Nefes T., Siang Ang, C. and Deravi, F. (2019). 'Understanding Conspiracy Theories', *Advances in Political Psychology*, 40(1), pp. 3–34. doi:10.1111/pops.12568.

Fenster, M. (2008). *Conspiracy Theories: Secrecy and Power in American Culture*. Minneapolis: University of Minnesota Press.

Fierke, K.M. (2013). *Political Self-Sacrifice: Agency, Body and Emotion in International Relations*. Cambridge: Cambridge University Press.

Goertzel, T. (1994). 'Belief in Conspiracy Theories', *Political Psychology*, 15(4), pp. 731–742.

Goldberg, R. (2001). *Enemies within: The Culture of Conspiracy in Modern America*. New Haven: Yale University Press.

Gray, M. (2010). *Conspiracy Theories in the Modern World. Sources and politics*. London: Routledge.

Hagemeister, M. (2008). 'The Protocols of the Elders of Zion: Between History and Fiction'. *New German Critique*, 35(1), pp. 83–95.

Hofstadter, R. (1965). *The Paranoid Style in American Politics, and Other Essays*. New York: Knopf.

ITU. (2018). *New ITU Statistics Show More than Half the World Is Now Using the Internet*. International Telecommunication Union. Available at: https://news.itu.int/itu-statistics-leaving-no-one-offline/ (Accessed: 25 February 2020).

Lafrance, A. (2020). 'The Prophecies of Q'. [Online] *The Atlantic*. Available at: https://www.theatlantic.com/magazine/archive/2020/06/qanon-nothing-can-stop-what-is-coming/610567/?fbclid=IwAR2x_mIbGK-p6rGkQ h8nyQCCN13HGRBfA3smLVtmZl94fEIuHnUSPgPNQXY (Accessed: 11 November 2020).

Laclau, E. (2005). *On Populist Reason*. London: Verso.

Basingstoke: Palgrave Macmillan, pp. 49–66.

Mazzoleni, G., Stewart, J. and Horsfield, B. (2003). *The Media and Neopopulism: A Contemporary Comparative Analysis*. Westport, CT: Praeger.

McLuhan, M. (1964). *Understanding of Media: The Extensions of Man*. New York: McGraw Hill.

Moffitt, B. and Tormey, S. (2014). 'Rethinking Populism: Politics, Mediatisation and Political Style', *Political Studies*, 62(2), pp. 381–397.

Moore, M. (2018). 'BBC Online Criticised for 'Pathetic' Clickbait', *The Times*, 15 January [Online]. Available at: https://www.thetimes.co.uk/article/bbc-online-criticised-for-pathetic-clickbait-9cfdxgf73 (Accessed: 28 February 2020).

Mudde, C. and Kaltwasser, C.R. (2017). *Populism: A Very Short Introduction*. Oxford: Oxford University Press.

Oberhauser, C. (2020) 'Simonini's letter: the 19th century text that influenced antisemitic conspiracy theories about the Illuminati'. *The Conversation*, 31 March [Online]. Available at: https://theconversation.com/simoninis-letter-the-19th-century-text-that-influenced-antisemitic-conspiracy-theories-about-the-illuminati-134635 (Accessed: 11 November 2020)

ONS. (2018). 'Office for National Statistics, Labour Force Survey', *Eurostat*. Available at: https://www.ons.gov.uk/businessindustryandtrade/itandinternet industry/bulletins/internetusers/2019 (Accessed: 25 February 2020).

Önnerfors A. and Krouwel A. (2021). *Europe: Continent of Conspiracies Conspiracy Theories in and about Europe*. London: Routledge.

Pagan, V. (2012). *Conspiracy theory in Latin Literature*. Austin: University of Texas Press.

Pickard, V. (2018). 'When Commercialism Trumps Democracy: Media Pathologies and the Rise of the Misinformation Society', in O. Bczkowski and Z. Papacharissi (eds.) *Trump and the Media*. Cambridge, MA: MIT Press, pp. 195–202.

Porter, L. (2005). *Who are the Illuminati?*. London: Collins & Brown.

Ramsay, G. and Robertshaw, S. (2018). *Weaponising News: RT, Sputnik and Targeted Disinformation*. King's College London: The Policy Institute. Available at: https://www.kcl.ac.uk/policy-institute/assets/weaponising-news.pdf.

Ritzer, G. and Jurgenson N. (2010). 'Production, Consumption, Prosumption: The nature of capitalism in the age of the digital "prosumer"'. *Journal of Consumer Culture*, 10(1), pp. 13–36.

Robb, A. (2017). 'Anatomy of a Fake News Scandal', *The Rolling Stone*, November 16. Available at: https://www.rollingstone.com/feature/anatomy-of-a-fake-news-scandal-125877/ (Accessed: 11 November 2020).

Roisman, J. (2006). *The rhetoric of conspiracy in Ancient Athens*. Berkeley: University of California Press.

Rosenthal, B. and Brito, E.P.Z. (2017). 'How Virtual Brand Community Traces May Increase Fan Engagement in Brand Pages', *Business Horizons*, 60, pp. 375–384.

RT. (2017). *'You Won't Scare Us': RT Guests Branded 'Useful Idiots' Voice Their Opinion* [Youtube]. Available at: https://www.youtube.com/watch?v=vP2hEI2Mcr8 (Accessed: 28 February 2020).

Silverman, C. (2016). 'This Analysis Shows How Viral Fake Election News Stories Outperformed Real News On Facebook', *Buzzfeed*, 16 November [Online]. Available at: https://www.buzzfeednews.com/article/craigsilverman/viral-fake-election-news-outperformed-real-news-on-facebook#. rtj0KJJGp (Accessed: 02 March 2020).

Silverman, C. and Singer-Vine, J. (2016). 'Most Americans Who See Fake News Believe It, New Survey Says', *Buzzfeed*, 6 December [Online]. Available at: https://www.buzzfeednews.com/article/craigsilverman/fake-news-survey#.kuo0e6QdV (Accessed: 02 March 2020).

Sommerlad, J. (2018). 'Fox News: How the Right-Wing Network Became One of America's Most Influential Political Voices', *The Independent*, 30 May [Online]. Available at: https://www.independent.co.uk/news/world/americas/us-politics/fox-news-network-america-trump-right-wing-republicans-rupert-murdoch-tv-station-a8375236.html (Accessed: 28 February, 2020).

Swami, V. (2012). 'Social psychological origins of conspiracy theories: the case of the Jewish conspiracy theory in Malaysia', *Frontiers in Psychology* 3, doi:10.3389/fpsyg.2012.00280.

Taggart, P. (2000). *Populism*. Buckingham: Open University Press.

Thallmann, K. (2019). *The Stigmatization of Conspiracy Theory since the 1950s. 'A Plot to Make us Look Foolish'*. London: Routledge.

Turcotte, J., York, C., Irving, J., Scholl, R.M. and Pingree, R.J. (2015). 'News Recommendations from Social Media Opinion Leaders: Effects on Media Trust and Information Seeking', *Journal of Computer-Mediated Communication*, 20(5), pp. 520–535.

Udani, A., Kimball, D.C. and Fogarty, B. (2018). 'How Local Media Coverage of Voter Fraud Influences Partisan Perceptions in the United States', *State Politics & Policy Quarterly*, 18, pp. 193–210. doi:10.1177/1532440018766907.

Vargo, C.J., Guo, L. and Amazeen, M.A. (2018). 'The Agenda-Setting Power of Fake News: A Big Data Analysis of the Online Media Landscape from 2014 to 2016', *New Media & Society*, 20(5), pp. 2028–2049.

Weeks, B.E. (2018). 'Media and Political Misperceptions', in B.G. Southwell, E.A. Thorson and L. Sheble (eds.) *Misinformation and Mass Audiences*. Austin: University of Texas Press, pp. 140–156.

Wong J.C. (2020). 'Facebook to ban QAnon-themed groups, pages and accounts in crackdown', *The Guardian*, 7 October [Online]. Available at: https://www.theguardian.com/technology/2020/oct/06/qanon-facebook-ban-conspiracy-theory-groups (Accessed: 11 November 2020).

Wood, M.J., Douglas, K.M. and Sutton, R.M. (2012). 'Dead and Alive: Beliefs in Contradictory Conspiracy Theories', *Social Psychological and Personality Science*, 3(6), 767–773. doi:10.1177/1948550611434786.

Yablokov, I. (2018). *Fortress Russia: Conspiracy Theories in the Post-Soviet World*. Cambridge: Polity.

Zannettou, S., Caulfield, T., De Cristofaro, E., Kourtellis, N., Leontiadis, I., Sirivianos, M. Stringhini, G. and Blackburn, J. (2017). 'The Web Centipede: Understanding How Web Communities Influence Each Other through the Lens of Mainstream and Alternative News Sources', *Proceedings of the 2017 Internet Measurement Conference (IMC'17)*, pp. 405–418 (14). Available at: https://doi.org/10.1145/3131365.3131390.

Zwierlein, C. (2020). 'Conspiracy theories in the Middle Ages and the Early Modern Period', in Knight P., and Butter M. (eds.) *Routledge Handbook of Conspiracy Theories*. London: Routledge, pp. 542–554.

Zwierlein, C. and Graaf, B. d. (2013). 'Security and conspiracy in modern history', *Historical Social Research*, 38(1), pp. 7–45.

2 'Question more'? The Kremlin's strategy behind RT

On the 31st of December 1999 Vladimir Putin, who had recently been appointed a Prime Minister, took over the office of President from the old and highly unpopular first Russian President, Boris Yeltsin. For many people in Russia this appointment of the young and promising politician was seen as the start of a new historical period. Yeltsin, whose popularity as a democratic leader was central to the destruction of the Soviet Union in 1991, lost support because of his economic reforms and an environment of corruption. Putin's rapid rise to power, his legalistic rhetoric and successful economic reforms in the early 2000s helped to shape his unquestionable support amongst the population, which allowed him to win the elections for the second time in 2004. On the foreign policy side Putin took a conciliatory approach, proposing increased strategic cooperation with the EU and providing practical support post 9/11 for counter-terrorism initiatives and for George W. Bush's 2001 military operation against Afghanistan (Hill, 2002). Russia's economic boom was seen by foreign investors as an opportunity not to be missed and even the first authoritarian touches of Putin's rule were not able to shake that impression (Sakwa, 2014).

Regime changes in the post-Soviet countries, that Moscow still considered its sphere of influence, however, were equally crucial for the evolution of Putin's authoritarianism, as domestic developments. First, the Georgian president Eduard Shevardnadze had been ousted by crowds led by the young neoliberal reformer Mikhail Saakashvili who would later become Russia's fiercest critic (Ó Beacháin and Polese, 2010). Second, in Ukraine the pro-Kremlin candidate Viktor Yanukovich lost to the West-oriented and nationalist Viktor Yushchenko in 2004, a strategically significant loss for the Kremlin (Wilson, 2014).

All these developments had one crucial outcome: Putin and his entourage had to do their best to protect their power in the country and simultaneously try to sustain reasonably good relations with the

West. For that purpose, deputy head of the Presidential Administration, Vladislav Surkov designed the concept of Russia as a sovereign democracy (Yablokov, 2018).

Russia as a global underdog

The point of Surkov's concept was to reshape the perception of the West in Russia by turning it from an enemy to a global competitor. 'The people have attained a new sense of sobriety. The romantic days are gone. We no longer have the feeling of being surrounded by enemies, but rather by competitors', said Surkov in an interview to the German *Der Spiegel* in 2005 (Klussmann and Mayr, 2005). That year was crucial for Russia's leadership and for setting the agenda for many years to come. At the start of the year Gleb Pavlovskii, a long-time adviser to the Kremlin, who personally witnessed the Kremlin's failure in Kyiv, returned to Moscow adamant that Russia would be the next on the US list of regimes to unseat. Given the forthcoming presidential elections of 2008, when Putin was supposed to leave the presidential office, it was crucial to create an ideological framework that would help to insulate Putin's entourage from the external pressure of democratisation. Consequently, Surkov, Pavlovskii and a team of PR advisers designed the idea of sovereign democracy that would incorporate populist claims of Putin being a representation of the 'people' of Russia. Although it would seem bizarre to perceive the president of the nuclear state and a leader of the G8 country a representation of ordinary people, this had resonated well on the domestic political stage.

As outlined in the previous chapter, populism is a way of uttering all sorts of conflicts that arise in a given society. The Kremlin channelled support to Putin by using a populist paradigm to present the conflicts that shook the collapsed empire and the desperate social inequality that ensued. The president was presented as a man of 'the people', who came to fulfil the demands of ordinary Russians both within Russia and abroad. To accomplish that mission, Surkov (2006) helped to re-format the way that the Russians have traditionally seen the West after 1917: from an enemy to a (suspect and dangerous) partner in a global game of politics, where Russia happens to be a weak player. Pragmatism in actions both within Russia and outside was advocated as a key to success. That rationalism helped shift the perception of the West and proved to be essential not only in bringing anti-Western conspiracy theories in Russia into the mainstream. The discourse of the West as a competitor opened numerous pathways for expressing criticism of the West – first and foremost of the US at the domestic Russian and global levels. Here the populist approach was manifested again: 'the people', represented by the Russian population and led by Putin, had to fight for equality on the global political stage where the hegemony of the US – the 'Other' – was portrayed as the key factor threatening Russia's global success. In other words, Surkov's populist idea of sovereign democracy divided the world between the 'people' who strived to become sovereign and the West who deprived them of this right when they assisted the Soviet collapse of 1991 (see Yablokov, 2018). Surkov thus presented a dualistic division of the world with Russia as the 'underdog' fighting the hegemony of the dangerous state that would do anything to keep the power (Laclau, 2005).

In the same fashion, the Kremlin's advisors, who designed the principles of sovereign democracy, attributed a global role to Putin himself. Amidst the debate around the famous Munich speech where Putin openly demonstrated the Kremlin's bid to challenge Western hegemony, Pavlovskii explained the role that Putin should play globally. He argued that US containment must be 'Russia's function', which would make the voice of the 'global people' heard (Pavlovskii, 2007). After Pavlovskii was sacked by his Kremlin counterparts, in his numerous interviews and books he admitted that the Kremlin worked hard to design a strategy that would place Russia as the leader of developing countries, a speaker on behalf of the global 'underdogs' who would rise against the 'New World Order' (Pavlovskii, 2014).

Soviet roots

The history of RT starts in the same year, 2005, when the Kremlin launched the campaign to promote the new state ideology. However, RT's roots are found deep in the history of the Soviet propaganda machine. The Bolshevik approach to the press and information saw the media as key to conveying the revolutionary message to the proletarians (Kenez, 1985). Once in power, the Bolsheviks, on the one hand, introduced censorship and banned all alternative press; on the other hand, they mobilised all available sources for agitation and propaganda as a means of generating social support for their actions. Propaganda was the crucial instrument of social mobilisation and even making the Soviet nation (see, Kenez, 1985; Lovell, 2015). In June 1941, just days after the Second World War began in the USSR, the Central Committee of the Communist Party of the Soviet Union set up an information office under the title *Sovinformbiuro* (Soviet information bureau) to update the population about the state of affairs on the front line. Essentially, a propaganda tool of the Soviet government, this bureau monopolised all information about war-related events (Berkhoff, 2012).

Sovinformbiuro was turned into the Agency of the Print Press 'the News' (*Agenstvo pechati Novosti or APN*) in 1961. APN's mission was to inform foreign audiences about the policies of the USSR and the life of the Soviet people. Its motto was 'Information for the benefit of the world, for the sake of peace between nations' (RIA Novosti, 2011). The agency was a hub of Soviet correspondents who covered foreign affairs; it was the core instrument by which the Soviet government could provide pro-Soviet information to various audiences across the world. For the Moscow Olympic Games in 1980, the Soviet government constructed a huge building in the centre of Moscow (Zubovskii boulevard 4) as APN's headquarter that hosted all media outlets related to Soviet foreign outreach activities. Needless to say, APN's actions were closely monitored and managed by high-ranking intelligence officers: APN's outreach activities were also part and parcel of the USSR's ideological war with the US during the Cold war (Poltoranin, 2010).

In 1987 Mikhail Gorbachev, the last leader of the Communist Party of the USSR, announced glasnost' – liberalisation of the media – for the sake of the 'purification' of Marxism (McNair, 1991). This policy allowed for an unprecedented freedom of expression, the likes of which journalists had not experienced since 1917. The Soviet government allowed journalists, whose wages it paid, to criticise its actions or demand opening archives that still held information that was hazardous for the legitimacy of the socialist regime. APN itself tried to push Gorbachev and perestroika further: according to APN's last director, Valentin Falin, the outlet used its facilities to translate and transmit articles about Soviet liberalisation in the Soviet bloc countries that local media considered too destabilising to reproduce (Rostova, 2015). In June 1990 a new Press Law was introduced that effectively ended the Soviet state monopoly on the press. For many media in the late USSR that was the start of a difficult time for survival, as state support slowly evaporated. APN, like other Soviet state-owned media outlets, was slowly disintegrating.

The post-Soviet U-turns

In 1992 editors-in-chief of leading Russian newspapers came to Boris Yeltsin to ask for financial support to sustain their printing facilities (Gatov, 2015b). At the same time many journalists and media managers worked hard to make extra money from hidden advertisement and other paid services beneficial to commercial partners, oligarchs-owners of their media or the Russian authorities (Schimpfössl and Yablokov, 2017b). In 1991 APN was turned into the Russian

Information Agency 'The News' (*RIA Novosti*) and in 1998 was merged with the state-owned broadcaster VGTRK occupying a minor share of the news making market. The media had to scrap for pennies to survive in the new capitalist Russia. The building at Zubovsky boulevard was rented out to various small companies, whilst salaries were often delayed.

It all changed in 2003 when Vladimir Putin appointed Svetlana Mironyuk as the head of the *RIA Novosti* wire service. The new media manager had spent her childhood in Soviet embassies across the world because Mironyuk's father was technical staff of the Ministry of Foreign Affairs. She was full of ideas and energy and, most importantly, had the right connections in the Russian government and the Presidential Administration. After fixing the economic problems of the agency, she re-launched *RIA Novosti* as a new media platform that in ten years' time outnumbered all non-television media in terms of brand awareness, audience and influence. *RIA Novosti* was the official Russian media to cover the Sochi Olympic Games in 2014 and gained popularity inside Russia for providing fairly objective information about politics and society. *RIA Novosti* launched a special news service RAPSI that covered court cases and streamed live videos from court rooms where the members of the opposition were on trial. Everyone could see the state-led injustice online.

That ability to cover what many state-affiliated media were not able to came because Mironyuk had excellent connections amongst the Kremlin's powerbrokers. Russian top media managers must have first-class connections not only with government executives and the Kremlin administration, they must also have a set of skills to navigate the murky waters of Russian politics. This system is in some ways reminiscent of the Soviet nomenklatura connections where access to limited services – such as top hospitals or foreign goods – provided a media manager with the reasons to abide by the system and his/her patrons (Gatov et al., 2017).

In the post-Soviet media, loyalty and access to money flows define individuals' places in the hierarchy: one must know exactly how to act and where to seek support in difficult circumstances. Media managers must sense what are the red lines in covering particular events, whom to choose as patrons, which financial gains to pursue and how to split revenues with the political stakeholders that can either protect them or promote them further on a career ladder (Schimpfössl and Yablokov, 2017a). The higher the position of the media manager in the state hierarchy, the higher the stakes of losing a career and the better the sense of appropriateness of what one is allowed to do, which is defined as *adekvatnost'* (Yablokov and Schimpfössl, 2020). All media managers in Russia develop the skill of *adekvatnost'* that helps them survive in the system of informal networks, and learn to self-censor themselves without necessarily diminishing the quality of the end product (Schimpfössl and Yablokov, 2014). As discussed elsewhere about Russian journalists,

> an outstanding journalist might be daring, flamboyant and quirky, but, in best traditions of Weberian patrimonial reciprocity, clearly knows how far to go, as overdoing such things or getting them wrong would be highly risky in the ever-changing political climate.
>
> (Schimpfössl and Yablokov, 2020)

What happened on the 9th of December 2013 was a showcase of how unpredictable the career of an excellent top media manager in Russia could be, should they fail to sense the boundaries of appropriateness in this system. After a meeting with editors and the minister of press, Mironyuk received a call from the head of the Presidential Administration Sergei Ivanov who informed her that she was fired. All top managers of *RIA Novosti*, who kept loyalty to Mironyuk, were also sacked. It turned out that on that day Vladimir Putin signed a decree that transformed *RIA Novosti* into the *International Information Agency* 'Rossiia Segodnia' (Russia Today) and appointed Margarita Simonyan its editor-in-chief and Dmitry Kiselev – a controversial state television presenter – as its head (Elder, 2013). Simonyan, who had been the head of RT since 2005, was technically Mironyuk's employee. However, it turned out that she had much stronger patrons in the government and the Presidential Administration than Mironyuk.

Simonyan's patron in the Presidential Administration is Aleksei Gromov, the head of Putin's media department and the person who personally manages the Kremlin's connections with the major media (Rubin et al., 2019). From the late 1990s Gromov's power over the media grew steadily: for instance, he organised the so-called Friday agenda planning meetings in the Kremlin where heads of all major Russian media were invited to be briefed on the forthcoming events from Putin's diary as well as suggestions on how to cover some news.[1] As Vasily Gatov notes, Simonyan was invited to these meetings in 2006 as Russia Today's representative and thus joined a loyal group of media managers grateful to Gromov for the chance to become a part of the media elite (Gatov, 2015b). Despite the fact that Russia Today's creation under the auspices of *RIA Novosti* was Gromov's idea, there are reports from former *RIA Novosti* employees that describe Gromov's frequent phone calls to Mironyuk, telling her off for the impartial coverage of the actions of the Russian opposition leaders or Putin's actions. As Mironyuk noted later, the number of conflicts was growing to the point where Gromov had escalated to all-out war against Mironyuk (Taratuta, 2015). The end of that war took place in December 2013, two months before the Sochi Olympic Games and a few months before Russia's invasion of Ukraine, when all Kremlin-related media switched to 24 hour propaganda mode. The Kremlin needed a more reliable manager to head its outreach activities and guarantee the Kremlin's strategy was being implemented bluntly and efficiently (Surganova, 2014).

Simonyan, a 25-year-old journalist in 2005 became RT's editor-in-chief thanks to her good relations with Kremlin patrons and for clearly knowing how to navigate Russian media politics. She was quickly transferred from the regional state television company in Krasnodar to Moscow, where in the course of a few months she became a senior correspondent who covered the terrorist attack in Beslan in 2004. Yet, the most significant appointment, which most probably started off her rapid career ascent, was her membership in the team of journalists that covered Vladimir Putin's daily routine for the state-owned media holding VGTRK. That is where she was able to increase her social capital and get to know both Gromov and Mikhail Lesin, Russia's media minister in the 2000s who were responsible for formatting the Russian media landscape in Kremlin-controlled terrain and worked hand in hand with Surkov (Gatov, 2015a). It is precisely these two who stood behind the creation of RT as one of the clear manifestations that Surkov's concept could be turned into a foreign policy tool. The leadership of this important Kremlin instrument additionally reinforced Simonyan's power inside Russia (Varshavchik, 2005).

'There is no such thing as objective reporting'

The launch of RT (originally as 'Russia Today') in December 2005 was one of the signs of the ambitions the Russian government had on the international stage. For their first years on the market, the channel recruited young Russians who were fluent in English and the formatting of the output allowed for discussion of the news from Russia as well as its culture or touristic attractions. In its first formative years, then, Russia Today had been one of the cultural outposts of Russia's soft power (Roxburgh, 2012). During the launch of the channel Mironyuk even stated that it would have a board of trustees that would consist of Russian and foreign journalists and which would monitor the impartiality of the channel (RIA Novosti, 2005).

Yet, in 2009 *Russia Today* was rebranded simply as RT. According to Simonyan, the change was made to ensure that the news of the channel would be appealing to a larger audience, beyond those interested in 'Russia', especially given the intention to reach English and Spanish speaking audiences in their home countries (Von Twickel, 2010). Yet, it seems plausible to argue that the key to understanding RT's evolution – from the media outlet that told stories about Russian culture (with a country name in its brand) to the aggressive 'ministry of information defence' under the bleak abbreviation – could be found in the August War in the South Caucasus in 2008 and how Russian actions had been reported internationally. The invasion of Russian forces – the first Russian military operation outside of its borders since Afghanistan in 1979 – was seen by many Western media as an act of aggression against the innocent former Soviet republic of Georgia. Despite RT quoting the most extreme line from Russia's domestic television, of Georgia's 'genocide' in South Ossetia, the dominant position of the non-Russian media was that Russia was at fault in starting that war (Birge and Chatterje-Doody, 2021). So, the team behind RT's re-launch had to find a way of breaking up this news monopoly with an alternative idea. What better way to create an ideological shield against Western intrusion into the Kremlin's interests than by re-casting the stories being told about unfolding events?

Simonyan's argument about why RT was reshaped is focussed on how dull the content of international channels is and how poorly they inform their audiences, who crave something different: 'mainstream western TV channels... show the same thing ... quite a lot of people in the world ... don't think that's how it should be, so it ... makes sense to make something for them. Obviously if our audience is [only] Kremlinologists and Russia watchers, then that's very few people' (Seddon, 2016). Her boss, Vladimir Putin, in 2013 put it differently and clearly: 'We wanted to break the monopoly of the Anglo-Saxon mass media in the global flow of information' (Audinet, 2017).

The approach that was followed after 2008 was to mix Surkov's vision of Russia as a global underdog and RT's mission to search for alternative stories, ideally in the 'backyard' of its Western counterparts.

> Everybody wants to know what is happening in their backyards... We decided ... to look for stories that are on the one hand extremely interesting, that can be breath-taking, fascinating for our audience, and on the other hand that have not been reported or hugely underreported in the mainstream media.
>
> (Kramer, 2010)

That combination was supposed to bring a greater audience to the stories allegedly unreported by the so-called 'mainstream media' and that would often be very critical of the US and Western European governments. Moreover, that approach is based on two premises: first, that 'people... understand that the whole truth cannot be told by Anglo-Saxon television channels' (Gabuev, 2012). And second, that 'there is no objectivity: there are as many approximations of the truth as there are potential voices' (Audinet, 2017). As the previous chapter's discussion of the contradictory trends in public trust, and the increased market incentives for subjective media content shows, this operating philosophy is well-suited to the contemporary global news media environment. What is more, the decision to trade the ethical principles shared by many professional media in the world for the ability to report anything that would stand the principle of 'ignored by the mainstream media' provides a fruitful basis for all sorts of claims (including conspiracy theories), used both by the radical left and radical right.

For the Kremlin that approach would mean that the international power that presents itself as a global 'underdog' would challenge the hegemony of the US and UK media that are seen as one big threat to the world. Hence, Russia and RT, in particular, make a claim to represent everyone who is irritated by the global dominance of the US. As discussed elsewhere,

> [t]he intellectual underpinnings of Surkov's ideas allowed RT to avoid marginalisation as a mouthpiece of the Kremlin by delivering to viewers alternative, but nevertheless meaningful, news. On the other hand, these ideas helped to carefully shape the news agenda in such a way that it would challenge the American and the European governments. A simultaneous adoption of arguments of left- and right-wing critics of the US gives RT leeway to adapt its narratives in relation to different audiences, thereby expanding its global influence.
>
> (Yablokov, 2015)

This is particularly the case, since RT tends to take those critical voices from within the societies in question (Chatterje-Doody and Crilley, 2019).

In situations when Russia hits the headlines, some UK and US politicians indeed overreact by blaming their opponents for working on behalf of the Kremlin. For instance, in 2015 Jeremy Corbyn was criticised by British newspapers for appearing on RT (Monkey, 2015).

Although this was not a major news item, Simonyan carefully picked up these claims and used them to justify how biased establishment politicians and the 'mainstream media' are towards RT and the Russian state: 'In June we interviewed Jeremy Corbyn. And two months later simultaneously *The Times, Independent* and *Telegraph*, and others follow their case start writing that Corbyn gave us an interview, which means he is working for Putin' (Surganova and Glikin, 2015). Simonyan's comments perfectly illustrate the 'outsider' element of RT's brand identity. She portrays RT as an outside voice that holds the establishment to account, and is attacked because of this.

The Crimean annexation and the following conflict in Eastern Ukraine certainly reinforced the role of the 'underdog' which Simonyan cherishes so much. When RT was criticised for biased coverage of the Ukraine conflict in 2014, Simonyan wrote the following blog entry:

> Every single day... the guys who work for us are told, 'You are liars, you are no journalists, you are the Kremlin propaganda mouthpiece...'... I can see very clearly why I ... work for a channel that stands alone (!) ... showing everybody the other side of the story.
>
> (Simonyan, 2014)

Conclusion

The populist approach taken by the Kremlin domestically has showed itself to be an efficient way of gaining and retaining popular support, enabling Putin to keep relatively high public approval ratings for more than 20 years. For approximately a decade Surkov has not been a presidential adviser, however, his visionary concept of the West as the competitive Other has spawned a whole generation of intellectuals and media personalities in Russia who blame the West for double standards and all sorts of crimes. Simonyan is amongst them: a young and ambitious journalist who quickly built a career as one of the Kremlin's most trusted spokespeople. The ideological instruments handed to Simonyan by Surkov's sovereign democracy were put into practice quite efficiently.

The 2010s have been a decade full of international crises in which Moscow often played a key role, causing international scandals, controversies and even wars. The shock experienced by the West from the annexation of Crimea, the wars in Eastern Ukraine and Syria as well as the hack of the Democratic party in the US in 2016 and the 2018 poisoning of the former double agent Skripal provided an abundance of reasons to blame the Kremlin for all sorts of misdeeds. In turn, this perfectly played into the hands of the Russian political elites, and RT as their mediator, that accused Western governments and the 'mainstream media' of Russophobia – a buzz word now often heard both from Putin and his numerous envoys.

They interpret Russophobia as the reaction of Western elites to Russia's growing political ambition and its ability to challenge the hypocrisy and double standards of the West through such instruments of international politics as RT (RT, 2015).

The consistent evolution of the channel from a minor international broadcaster in the 2000s into the 'propaganda bullhorn' of the mid-2010s required strategic thinking on the part of the Kremlin and the channel's management (LoGiurato, 2014). Following the failure to report the Moscow perspective on the conflict in South Ossetia the channel very quickly was turned to reveal 'the skeletons' in the closet of the US, the UK and other European powers where RT opened additional branches throughout the 2010s. The Kremlin has chosen to keep the pressure on the West with its contrasting readings of contemporary political conflicts, as demonstrated by the 2008 definition of RT as the Russian government's strategic media company and the 2013 restructuring of *RIA Novosti* as *Rossiya Segodnya* under the loyal leadership of Simonyan (RBK, 2008). In replacing Mironyuk with Simonyan, the Kremlin proved willing to dismiss a media manager who had proved her efficiency, in exchange for appointing a more loyal one able to sustain the smokescreen of Russia's media operations amidst international political disasters such as the Crimea annexation or the Syrian Civil War. However, one of the most important battlefields proved to be the US market, where RT launched operations in 2010.

Note

1 It is these meetings that often are considered to be the place where the media outlets receive blacklists of people not be invited or interviewed.

References

Audinet, M. (2017). 'RT, Russia's Voice to the World', *Le Monde Diplomatique*. Available at: https://mondediplo.com/2017/04/08RT (Accessed: 13 November 2020).

Berkhoff, K.C. (2012). *Motherland in Danger: Soviet Propaganda during World War II*. Cambridge, MA: Harvard University Press.

Birge, L. and Chatterje-Doody, P.N. (2021). 'Russian Public Diplomacy: Questioning Certainties in Uncertain Times', in P. Surowiec and I. Manor (eds.) *Public Diplomacy and the Politics of Uncertainty*. London: Palgrave, pp. 171–195.

Chatterje-Doody, P.N. and Crilley, R. (2019). 'Populism and Contemporary Global Media: Populist Communication Logics and the Co-construction of Transnational Identities' in D. MacDonald, D. Nabers and F. Stengel (eds.) *Populism and World Politics: Exploring Inter- and Transnational Dimensions*. London: Palgrave Macmillan, pp. 73–99.

Elder, M. (2013). 'Kremlin 'Liquidates' Leading News Agency as Press Crackdown Grows', *Buzzfeed*, 9 December [Online]. Available at: https://www.buzzfeednews.com/article/miriamelder/kremlin-liquidates-leading-news-agency-as-press-crackdown-gr (Accessed: 13 November 2020).

Gabuev, A. (2012). 'Net nikakoi ob'ektivnosti', *Kommersant*, 12 April [Online]. Available at: https://www.kommersant.ru/doc/1911336 (Accessed: 13 November 2020).

Gatov, V. (2015a). 'How the Kremlin and the Media Ended up in Bed Together', *The Moscow Times*, 11 March [Online]. Available at: https://www.themoscowtimes.com/2015/03/11/how-the-kremlin-and-the-media-ended-up-in-bed-together-a44663 (Accessed: 13 November 2020).

Gatov, V. (2015b). *Putin, Maria Ivanovna from Ivanovo and Ukrainians on the Telly*. London: Henry Jackson Society.

Gatov, V., Schimpfössl, E. and Yablokov, I. (2017). 'From Soviet to Russian Media Managers', *Russian Politics*, 2(1), pp. 7–31.

Hill, F. (2002). *Putin and Bush in Common Cause? Russia's View of the Terrorist Threat after September 11. (The Shock Wave Abroad)*. Brookings Institute. Available at: https://www.brookings.edu/articles/putin-and-bush-in-common-cause-russias-view-of-the-terrorist-threat-after-september-11/ (Accessed: 13 November 2020).

Kenez, P. (1985) *The Birth of the Propaganda State: Soviet Methods of Mass Mobilization 1917–1929*. Cambridge: Cambridge University Press.

Klussmann, U. and Mayr, W. (2005). 'Interview with Kremlin boss Vladislav Surkov: 'The West Doesn't Have to Love Us'', *Spiegel*, [Online]. Available at: http://www.spiegel.de/international/spiegel/spiegel-interview-with-kremlin-boss-vladislav-surkov-the-west-doesn-t-have-to-love-us-a-361236.html (Accessed: 13 November 2020).

Kramer, A. (2010). 'Russian Cable Station Plays to the U.S', *The New York Times*, 23 August [Online]. Available at: https://www.nytimes.com/2010/08/23/business/media/23russiatoday.html?pagewanted=1&_r=2 (Accessed: 13 November 2020).

Laclau, E. (2005). *On Populist Reason*. London: Verso.

LoGiurato, B. (2014). 'RT Is Very Upset with John Kerry for Blasting Them as 'Putin's Propaganda Bullhorn'', *Business Insider*, 25 April [Online]. Available at: https://www.businessinsider.com/john-kerry-rt-propaganda-bullhorn-russia-today-2014-4 (Accessed: 13 November 2020).

Lovell, S. (2015). *Russia in the Microphone Age. A History of Soviet Radio, 1919–1970*. Oxford: Oxford University Press.

McNair, B. (1991). *Glasnost, P.erestroika and the Soviet Media*. London: Routledge.

Media Monkey. (2015). 'British Press Putin the Boot into Corbyn?' *The Guardian*, 13 August [Online]. Available at: https://www.theguardian.com/media/mediamonkeyblog/2015/aug/13/british-press-putin-the-boot-into-corbyn (Accessed: 13 November 2020).

Ó Beacháin, D. and Polese A. (eds.) (2010). *The Colour Revolutions in the Former Soviet Republics: Successes and Failures*. London: Routledge.

Pavlovskii, G. (2007). 'Rol' Putina i dal'she budet igrat'' Putin', *Moskovskie novosti*, [Online]. Available at: http://novchronic.ru/860.htm (Accessed: 13 November 2020).

Pavlovskii, G. (2014). 'Kreml: ot konservativnoi povestki – k revolutsii', *Russkii zhurnal*, [Online]. Available at: http://russ.ru/Mirovaya-povestka/Kreml-ot-konservativnoj-politiki-k-revolyucii (Accessed: 13 November 2020).

Poltoranin, M. (2010). *Vlast' v trotilovom ekvivalente. Nasledie tsaria Borisa*. Moscow: Eksmo.

RBK. (2008). 'Pravitel'stvo RF prinialo perechen' sistemoobrazuiushcikh predpriiatii', *RBK*, 25 December [Online]. Available at: http:/top.rbc.ru/economics/25/12/2008/271243.shtml (13 November 2020).

RIA Novosti. (2011). 'Istoriia agentstva pechati 'Novosti'', *RIA Novosti*, 1 March [Online]. Available at: https://ria.ru/20110301/340763479.html (Accessed: 13 November 2020).

RIA Novosti. (2005). 'V Rossii uchrezhden angloiazychnyi kanal Russia Today', *RIA Novosti*, 7 June [Online]. Available at: https://ria.ru/20050607/40484314.html (Accessed: 13 November 2020).

Rostova, N. (2015). 'Gorbachev dal dobro, i eto glavnoe, na to, chtoby liudi zhili svoim umom. No dlia togo, chtoby zhit' svoim umom, dolzhen byt' dustup k informatsii', *Gorbymedia*. Available at: https://gorbymedia.com/interviews/falin (Accessed: 13 November 2020).

Roxburgh, A. (2012). *The Strongman: Vladimir Putin and the Struggle for Russia*. London: I.B. Tauris.

RT. (2015). 'Why We Love to Hate Russia? European Writer Guy Mettan Enlightens RT', *RT*, 26 May [Online]. Available at: https://www.rt.com/op-ed/262233-russophobia-guy-mettan-book/ (Accessed: 14 October 2020).

Rubin, M., Zholobova, M. and Badanin, R. (2019). 'Master of Puppets: The Man Behind the Kremlin's Control of the Media', *Proekt*, 5 June [Online]. Available at: https://www.proekt.media/en/portrait-en/alexey-gromov-eng/ (Accessed: 13 November 2020).

Sakwa, R. (2014). *Putin and the Oligarch: The Khodorkovsky-Yukos Affair*. London: I.B. Tauris.

Schimpfössl, E. and Yablokov, I. (2014). 'Coercion or Conformism? Censorship and Self-censorship among Russian Media Personalities and Reporters in the 2010s', *Democratizatsiya: The Journal of Post-Soviet Democratization*, 20(2), pp. 295–312.

Schimpfössl, E. and Yablokov, I. (2017a). 'Media Elites in post-Soviet Russia and Their Strategies of Success', *Russian Politics*, 2(1), pp. 32–53.

Schimpfössl, E. and Yablokov, I. (2017b). 'Power Lost and Freedom Relinquished: Russian Journalists Assessing the First post-Soviet Decade', *The Russian Review*, 76, pp. 524–539.

Schimpfössl, E. and Yablokov, I. (2020). 'Post-socialist Self-Censorship: Russia, Hungary, Latvia', *European Journal of Communication*, 35, pp. 29–45.

Seddon, M. (2016). 'Lunch with the FT: Kremlin Media Star Margarita Simonyan', *The Financial Times*, 29 July [Online]. Available at: https://www.ft.com/content/7987e5c2-54b0-11e6-9664-e0bdc13c3bef (Accessed: 13 November 2020).

Simonyan, M. (2014). 'About Abby Martin, Liz Wahl and Media Wars', *RT*, 6 March [Online]. Available at: https://www.rt.com/op-ed/about-liz-wahl-media-wars-126/ (Accessed: 13 November 2020).

Surganova, E. (2014). 'Agentstvo bez petukhov: kak RIA Novosti prevrashchalos' v 'Rossiiu segodnia'', *Forbes*, 10 December [Online]. Available at: https://www.forbes.ru/kompanii/internet-telekom-i-media/275199-agentstvo-bez-petukhov-kak-ria-novosti-prevrashchalos-v-ros (Accessed: 13 November 2020).

Surganova, E. and Glikin, M. (2015). 'Margarita Simonyan – RBK: 'Liberal'noe SMI kak raz moe'', *RBK*, 14 September [Online]. Available at: https://www.rbc.ru/interview/technology_and_media/14/09/2015/55dc76c19a7947b3a3deed3f (Accessed: 14 November 2020).

Surkov, V. (2006). 'Natsionalizatsiia budushchego', *Ekspert*, [Online]. Available at: http://expert.ru/expert/2006/43/nacionalizaciya_buduschego/ (Accessed: 13 November 2020).

Taratuta, Y. (2015). 'Svetlana Mironiuk: 'Ia tochno znala, chto nikogda bol'she ne bdud rabotat' na gosudarstvo'', *Forbes*, 30 October [Online]. Available at: https://www.forbes.ru/forbes-woman/karera/304331-svetlana-mironyuk-ya-tochno-znayu-chto-nikogda-bolshe-ne-budu-rabotat-na (Accessed: 13 November 2020).

Varshavchik, S. (2005). 'Zhenskoe litso propagandy', *Nezavisimaia gazeta*, 8 August [Online]. Available at: https://www.ng.ru/politics/2005-06-08/2_propaganda.html?id_user=Y (Accessed: 13 November 2020).

Von Twickel, N. (2010). 'Russia Today Courts Viewers with Controversy. Russia Beyond the Headlines', *Russia Beyond the Headlines*, 23 March [Online]. Available at: https://www.rbth.com/articles/2010/03/23/230310_rt.html (Accessed: 13 November 2020).

Wilson, A. (2014). *Ukraine Crisis: What It Means for the West*. New Haven, CT: Yale University Press.

Yablokov, I. (2015). 'Conspiracy Theories as Russia's Public Diplomacy Tool: The Case of 'Russia Today (RT)', *Politics*, 35(3–4), pp. 301–315.

Yablokov, I. (2018). *Fortress Russia: Conspiracy Theories in the post-Soviet Space*. Cambridge: Polity.

3 The world according to the Truthseekers

'Here is some hard truth' – says Daniel Bushell at the start and the end of each episode of 'The Truthseeker'. This show, which aired on a weekly basis from 2013 to summer 2015, cast doubt on numerous events in the US's past and on the state's current policies. In 2015, the British media regulator, Ofcom, ruled that two episodes of *The Truthseeker* broadcast summer 2014 had breached broadcasting rules. In the most serious case, the presenter claimed that the BBC had staged a chemical attack in Syria, thus legitimising the military invasion into the country. Ofcom ruled that the programme's coverage of this story was 'materially misleading' – the most significant category of breach – and ordered the network to broadcast a summary of the regulator's findings (Ofcom, 2014). *The Truthseeker* aired similar claims with regard to the raging Civil War in the centre of Kyiv, Ukraine, where protesters clashed with the police and anonymous snipers fatally shot dozens of people (Schwartz, 2018). According to Bushell, these clashes constituted a 'typical false flag operation' by the US government, aimed at overthrowing the Ukrainian government regime of Viktor Yanukovich. Filled with conspiratorial allegations, *The Truthseeker* represented a clear example of the kind of naked engagement with conspiracy theories that RT practised in the early 2010s. Since the conflict was still unfolding at the time (and all facts were not reliably established), Ofcom would not pass judgement on whether RT's account here had been materially misleading. However, for failing to adequately represent the Ukrainian position, Ofcom (2015) found that RT had breached the requirement for 'due impartiality' in reporting this matter of ongoing political controversy.

The channel quickly responded to finding its programmes under such strict scrutiny. Prior to Ofcom's action, RT had already cancelled *The Truthseeker* and removed all historical episodes from its website (Ofcom, 2015, p. 11), which may have contributed to the relatively lenient sanctions ultimately imposed for these breaches. Furthermore, producers of the channel seemed to change their approach. First, RT gradually moved to a more accurate application of conspiracy theories, yet regularly sowing doubts about the actions of Russia's geopolitical rival: the US. In September 2017 the channel launched a new show, *The World According to Jesse*, hosted by a famous conspiracy theorist Jesse Ventura, who had previously worked for three seasons on the show, 'Conspiracy theories with Jesse Ventura' on US cable network TruTV. Second, RT employed 'respected' speakers and presenters to improve the image of the channel. These included former British politicians Alex Salmond and George Galloway as well as US TV presenter Larry King. Thus, Ventura, a former Minnesota governor and TV celebrity, became one more famous face to add to RT's portfolio of presenters. Despite its slightly different format and length, Ventura's show occupied the same niche as *The Truthseeker*, ranting about corrupt elites, mainstream media and the militant hawks in Washington whose guiding principle is to destroy the world and profit from this catastrophe. Its output displayed one major difference, however: it avoided open conspiratorial and unverifiable allegations.

The clearly anti-US messages of both programmes, wrapped in conspiratorial packaging, are the most overt example of RT's engagement with conspiracy theories and offer an illustrative vantage point for observing how and why the strategy of employing conspiracy theories changed over time. Both shows clearly demonstrate RT's skill at tapping into the US conspiratorial environment and skilfully tying it up with events of contemporary political relevance.

The Truthseeker's pilot episode dealt with 9/11 conspiracy theories: it is a discussion of the alternative accounts of the 9/11 terrorist attacks that present the US government as an instigator of this human tragedy, in order to provide justification for the invasion of Iraq. Bushell's assumption is that the US potential military intervention of Syria will be performed in a similar manner. Ventura's show, launched on 11 September 2017 (emblematic in itself), spent the whole first episode discussing the US press coverage of the possible collusion between then-Presidential candidate Donald Trump with representatives of the Russian state. It was claimed and later partially proven that Trump's closest aides had contacts with Russian diplomats and other citizens that they preferred to keep secret from investigators (American Constitutional Society, 2019), though no collusion was proven on the part of Trump himself. Ventura's presentation of the story was one of a plot between the mainstream media and the 'corrupt elites' seeking to undermine the electoral success of a political outsider. Within Ventura's narrative, the constant cycle of US interference in foreign elections since the Second World War, and the lack of evidence that the Iraqi government of Saddam Hussein had ever possessed the purported weapons of mass destruction that were used to justify the 2003 allied invasion, were both presented as clear examples of the hypocrisy of US political elites. Hence, as Ventura contended, the anti-Russian stance was driven by the greed and cynicism of the US government.

The focus on the 9/11 tragedy and the Iraq War thus framed the reading of US policies as part of a US-led plot to create a unipolar world under its command. By implication, Russia stands as a part of the global resistance – a figurehead for those ready to speak the truth about the dangers of the US-led world order. Opposing Russia is the US government, that, according to numerous RT reports, stood behind the 9/11 terrorist attacks that opened the way for the US military to invade countries abroad. In 2010, when RT launched its broadcasting in the US under the name RT America, one of the first stories published on its website was the article: '911 questions to the US government about 9/11' (Yablokov, 2015). It was soon removed from the website, but as we shall see shortly, this conspiracy theory is important in shaping RT's conspiratorial narratives.

'Seek truth from facts': undermining the status quo

From its first episode, Bushell's *The Truthseeker* takes a pro-active stance on uncovering the US government's plots and cover-ups against the American people. The tag line used by the presenter at the end of every show ('seek truth from facts') is emblematic: the claim that this programme can uncover government and elite plots against ordinary Americans helps to sow doubt amongst the audience of the channel. The categories of 'truth' and 'trust' are crucial here to understand the rationale behind the programme's agenda.

Anthony Giddens defines trust as 'confidence in the reliability of a person or a system, regarding a given set of outcomes and events' (Giddens, 1991). Trust is a product of rationally assessing the consequences of actions of various social agents. People who 'trust' other people or institutions do so because they perceive their actions as reliable. Any risk they take is well calculated and can be checked by objective methods. When it comes to the discussion of whether, e.g. the government can be trusted, history provides manifold examples of failures or cover-ups that reinforce suspicion of the good faith of governmental institutions (see Lewis, 2008). Even if these institutions aim at achieving transparency and better ways of operating, people will still assess them based on images and concepts that have long historical pedigrees and which promote a suspicious relationship towards power (Sanders and West, 2003). In the case of the US, this historical pedigree is rich and provides a lot of precedent for challenging the government's possible good intentions.

From the onset of the American republic, the balance of power in the country depended on suspicion of what the ruling elite was trying to achieve. Indeed, fears about corruption and cover-ups stretch all the way back to contemporaneous suggestions that George Washington had autocratic ambitions. This generates a fruitful ground for constant suspicions and various enthusiasts often share the 'truth' about the government's plot to strip the nation of sovereignty, curtail people's rights and shift the power from the people to the heart of this sinister conspiracy (like Washington or Wall Street). This search for truth is central to conspiracy theorists' actions: uncovering plots organised by the all-powerful agencies is the core of their activity. This 'truth' is supposed to illuminate the 'real' workings of power in society and also, as psychologists note, each version of truth offers a way to comprehend what is behind the belief in conspiracy theories (Raab et al., 2013).

For partisan politicians it is essential to speak truth to conspiracy, even when the conspiratorial version of events is just one (and not the main) plausible option (Muirhead and Rosenblum, 2016). Yet, when elected politicians or other state actors are caught lying, this dramatically reduces their credibility to debunk conspiracy theories or make people believe less in the conspiratorial option. The secrets, half-truths and blatant lies that often accompany the political process, create a toxic atmosphere of distrust and increase the popularity of conspiracy theories. It is precisely this atmosphere that *The Truthseeker* so skilfully uses, and the first episode of the show encapsulates all of the strategies that RT applies to handle conspiracy theories.

The array of conspiracy theories accusing the government, big corporations and mainstream media of stripping Americans of their rights and waging an unseen war against individuals creates an alternative 'regime of truth' in the Foucaldian sense (Weir, 2008). The starting topic of the series of these programmes – the 9/11 conspiracy – is also indicative: Bushell taps into the abundant culture of the Truthers movement – the group of believers that 9/11 was an inside job perpetrated by the US government in order to spread US hegemony to the Middle East and across the world (Kay, 2011).

The narrative of the Truthers community that sprang up and blossomed from the mid-2000s challenges every bit of the official version of the events of 9/11, suggesting a series of secret operations to explode the buildings and present what happened as a terrorist attack. There were no terrorists, no planes, no conspiracy of radical Islamist terrorists and even no Bin Laden: all that happened was a carefully planned and orchestrated operation by the US government ruled by the neoconservatives and the military-industrial complex. The further attempt to provide an investigation into the 9/11 events was a part of the big lie to cover the truth (Griffin, 2005).

The pilot episode (00) of *The Truthseeker* begins with a story about a billboard at Times Square in New York that asked: 'Did you know a third tower fell on September 11?' [1] The advert posted by the group 'Architects and Engineers for 9/11 Truth' called the public to question the validity of the official version of 9/11 (Merlan, 2013). *The Truthseeker* endorsed several scientists who were activists in the 9/11 Truther movement, stressing their leading character in the investigation and the academic status of authors of alternative accounts. Bushell and his guests noted that the official account of events had already changed under pressure and referred to the report on the reasons for WTC7's collapse.

The next block of the episode gave the floor to accounts of ordinary passers-by who allegedly witnessed the explosions in the WTC, which the media never reported on. Then, the presenter switched to criticism of the US media celebrity Rachel Maddow. She had publicly branded the 9/11 truthers as conspiracy theorists, including Bob McIlvaine, whose son died in the terrorist attack (Steele, 2013). McIlvaine, in an interview with Bushell that started with the question: 'How do you feel first losing a son and now being portrayed as the bad guy' claimed that the US mainstream media would never allow the truth of 9/11 to be released, accusing media owners of hiding the truth from the people. McIlvaine essentially argued that a 9/11 cover-up had led to the Iraqi and Syrian war campaigns of the US government, causing the grief of innocent people around the world. The events of September 2001 and the current global agenda of the US military have been closely tied together underpinning the US global imperialist ambitions as a source of global conflicts that opened space for various conspiracy allegations.

Within just the first few minutes of the pilot *The Truthseeker* episode all the key elements of RT's agenda have been demonstrated: the corrupt US government that covers up its crimes, mainstream media that will not report the truth because of their owners' will, the US as a source of suffering of people across the world and the handpicked expert knowledge that serves to endorse necessary allegations without subverting the presenter's line. The stress on alternative voices that are called 'conspiracy theorists' by the mainstream media falls within RT's claim to grant a platform to the dissident voices willing to speak the truth, regardless of the consequences.

The US government as a ruthless killer

The criticism of US domestic and foreign policies is one of three sides of the triangle of RT's core content. In order to convince audiences that the US government is corrupt, untrustworthy and capable of committing any possible crime, *The Truthseeker* unashamedly takes one side, then picks up and mashes together all corroborating evidence and conspiratorial allusions. This strategy creates the necessary background to planting doubts which will then provide legitimacy for conspiracy theories and provoke criticism of Russia's geopolitical opponent.

The subsequent episodes (01 and 02) of the programme are devoted to lobbyism, the corrupt Obama administration and the US government drone programme that is a threat to ordinary Americans. Unable to interview Obama himself, Bushell projects a possible interview with the re-elected president onto a Lego game where 'Darth Obama' is impersonated by Darth Vader, the villain from the Star Wars trilogy. He admits that the US bombs foreign countries, its soldiers die and that Guantanamo will continue, despite the promise to shut it down immediately after being elected. The presenter accuses Obama of running a drone programme that kills Americans and foreigners daily, which is also at the root of violence and racism in the US (The Truthseeker, 2016b).

These drone scares, popular amongst US government critics, are very similar to the conspiracy theories of the New World Order that appeared in the 1990s in the US. Back then black helicopters had been interpreted as evidence of the omnipotent power of the New World Order conspirators to observe any actions of dissent. The American conspiracy culture of the 1990s had numerous references to the black helicopters that fly over the US and represented evil forces ready to take over the country (Keith, 1994). These fears of black helicopters have been advantageous to illustrate the existence of a government conspiracy because, on the one hand, helicopters are real, unlike UFOs, and the government does have a lot of these machines. On the other hand, they are elusive as they have no numbers to trace ownership. Thus, 'the believer or viewer can project onto them whatever manner of villainy seems most suitable, making them an all-purpose object for fears and anxieties' (Barkun, 2003, p. 71). The drone scares seem likely to resonate with the same people who shared the fears of the black helicopters 20 years ago. In 2012, in conversation with the conspiracy theorist Alex Jones, another far-right activist, Joseph Farah, referred to the drones that allegedly watched his property, thus extending the monitoring of dissent onto private space. According to Jones, it was proof of 'an outside globalist takeover' and another step in the governmental programme of population control (Nelson, 2012).

The Truthseeker continued this logic in Episode 08 by showing how drones – an instrument of US military domination – came to punish the American people (The Truthseeker, 2016c). Drones allegedly monitor Americans' private property, thus demonstrating the 'police state mentality' of the US government. Jason Leopold, an author at the conspiracy theories website *Truthout*, alleged that the US is already a police state and that everyone claiming this is labelled a conspiracy theorist by the mainstream media. Amidst the scandal around Edward Snowden's whistleblowing, which took place same year, these allegations appeared more plausible (Greenwald et al., 2013). The rest of the guests, civil activists or journalists, confirmed that the government breaches the Constitution and breaks basic human rights by intervening into private life. Civil activist Kade Crockford of the American Civil Liberties Union described how the police and other private companies can abuse their clearance to access private data and can follow innocent citizens. 'In the USSA the TV is watching you' – Bushell concludes the programme (The Truthseeker, 2016c).

The 'imperialist' dimension of US policies is another way of showing how crooked and dictatorial the US government is. Episode 07 discusses Hillary Clinton and her 'cold-blooded policies' that killed the US ambassador and several other Americans in 2011 as well as triggered violence in Libya (The Truthseeker, 2016e). Her laughter over the deaths in Libya, recorded on camera during the interview, shows how merciless the Secretary of State is (The Truthseeker, 2016d). We are told that the government is preparing to invade Iran, using CIA-controlled Hollywood companies to prepare the population for this attack. Scenes from 'Argo' and 'the Night of the Dead' are used to demonstrate how Hollywood prepares Americans for mass murders of Iranians: they should be seen as zombies not human beings, which will allow the US to commit war crimes (The Truthseeker, 2016f). Allegedly, the US has done this across Syria, Egypt and Thailand, sending snipers to help replace incumbents with puppets (The Truthseeker, 2016h). Those who uncover the war crimes become dissidents and are severely punished by the state (The Truthseeker, 2016g).

To make the argument about US imperialism even more relevant to US audiences, Kevin Barrett suggests, in a conspiratorial way, that the US 'colonialist policies' are funded from the taxpayer's pockets:

> It's the military-industrial complex who is colonising the American people, draining its economic resources and stealing from it, looting it!. ... these policies are imposed by ... the military-industrial complex, or [by]... banksters: the Rothschilds and the Rockefellers... who try to build the New World Order and the global government.
>
> (The Truthseeker, 2016h)

Who controls America?

The sinister centre of conspiracy against the Americans is (unsurprisingly) found at Wall Street and the Federal Reserve Commission where 'faceless' bankers and big corporations together with the corrupt federal government do anything to enslave Americans. In a particularly conspiratorial fashion the programme engaged with the utterly millennial conspiracy theories that demonise big business and the government that protects it: the references to the 2008 economic crisis that hit several generations of Americans hard provide a necessary background to legitimise conspiracy theories and will likely resonate with young viewers of the channel, who still remember the crisis.

At the onset of Episode 01 the show discussed the impact of genetically modified organisms (GMO) and the role of Monsanto corporation in spreading its production across the world using US diplomatic resources. The Monsanto conspiracy theories are abundant and allege of a plot to spread hazardous genetically modified food across the world (Norwood et al., 2014). It is also a good starting point to address various audiences across the US political spectrum: in the end everyone depends on the food they eat. Showing a map that illustrates the spread of Monsanto's products, the presenter notes that almost all countries, except Russia, have planted genetically modified seeds. Bushell contends that Monsanto 'dodges' GMO checks and pays politicians to prevent any bans on GMO. In episode 17, entitled 'Eugenics now', we learn that the global financial elite, represented by Bill Gates, has a plan to 'cut the world's population' by spreading GM food in the poorest areas of the world, thus targeting and slowly killing the most socially deprived people. In a style of moral panic, the presenter suggests that Monsanto stands behind a conspiracy to control 100% of the food produced in the world, which the government does not plan to prevent (The Truthseeker, 2016i). This is related, according to the host, to the lobbying potential of big business, which financially controls the political elite in the US.

One of the ways that RT engages with the booming conspiracy culture in the US is by strongly linking to 'New World Order' related conspiracy theories, which claim that the global elite is plotting to destroy excessive population (Rae, 2014). Raising the issue of the possibly modified and hazardous food is a way of addressing audiences who can potentially be having a moral panic about that issue. Consequently, for them RT can become a reliable source of information and an outlet that speaks truth against all odds. Another way is to bring up traditional conspiratorial allegations – such as the conspiracy of bankers – that have a long pedigree and are established in the imagination of the US public. And yet, after the 2008 financial crisis, it became even more pronounced and built upon solid evidence (Crosthwaite et al., 2014). The fact that very few people bore responsibility for the global economic crisis provided enough evidence to claim a secret agreement between the government and the Wall Street bankers (see, for instance, Sorkin, 2010).

Such figures as the Rothschilds and the Rockefellers – central to the New World Order conspiracy theories – are rarely mentioned by the programme's host or their experts. Instead, any discussion of the US financial industry includes references to Wall Street, big banks but most importantly has no references to concrete people. This anonymity not only protects the channel from legal action but helps authors to blur the line between the actual allegations and allusions to conspiracies and create the fear or the total suspicion of who can be a plotter. Ultimately, the threat that the government poses to ordinary Americans is driven by the unlimited greed of corporations and banks. Referring to a timeline showing financial crises in the past, Bushell and his guests contend that the banks are at the root of social problems and that the control of US banks over political systems across the world is unlimited. Apart from getting profit from Americans – dead or alive – and creating an enormous national debt, the banks have always plotted against ordinary Americans (The Truthseeker, 2016j).

Another way to address social problems in the US – such as school shootings, obesity or low education – is by blaming big corporations for plotting against American youth. 'The junk-food conspiracy' is discussed in the third episode of *The Truthseeker* where Bushell explained how big corporations poison the nation by selling high-fructose, cheap food to millions of Americans. It is a matter of historical record that during 1950s, US public debate about healthy eating suggested that sugar was less dangerous than salt (Leslie, 2016). Yet, Bushell uses that fact to build a theory that big food brands use adverts to make the nation addicted to toxic foods, whilst the elites, like the New York Mayor Michael Bloomberg, help to promote these policies (The Truthseeker, 2016k). In a fashion which bears clear similarities to Soviet anti-US propaganda, Bushell argues in episode 29 that the 50% of the US state budget is allocated to military spending, and only 6% to education (The Truthseeker, 2016l). This results in the high price of US education, prostitution amongst young Americans who need to pay for college and, what is more dangerous, reliance on pharmaceuticals that affect brain activity.

In episode 6, Bushell argues that school shootings in the last decade could be caused by the drugs prescribed by doctors. The government wages 'Pharmageddon' on American children, claims Bushell: whilst the government approved the use of hard pharmaceuticals to children, 'Big Pharma' hid the deaths the medication caused. 'No regime in the history of this world has ever tried such a deadly mass drug experiment on its own people. The full effect will be seen on today's children in fifty years' time when our current leaders are not around to face the consequences', concludes Bushell at the end of the episode (The Truthseeker, 2016m).

The twist of the causes of the school shootings is notable: if RT took a clear stance to ban fire arms in the US that would make it look like the mainstream US liberal media – a step unacceptable for the underdog broadcaster that constantly accuses mainstream media of all possible crimes. Instead, the programme took an unconventional step and focussed on the corporate plot against the children, thus avoiding the criticism of the far-right, who could be a potential audience of the channel and, at the same time sounding plausible to the far-left.

The so called 'mainstream media' is undoubtedly RT's central target. Several programmes criticise mainstream media as the root cause of the US's domestic and international problems. For *The Truthseeker* the so called 'mainstream media' is the crucial element of the anti-American conspiracy of the elites. Americans can never receive objective information, because the elites control the information flow (The Truthseeker, 2016n, 2016o). Episode 10, tellingly entitled 'Presstitutes', opens with the statement that the media are in 'bed with those they are supposed to be grilling' (The Truthseeker, 2016n). Joe Farah, the contributor who had alluded that government drones were conspiring against him, contends that all big media are 'eating out of Obama's hand' and will change their editorial direction at 'the snap of his' fingers. Based on the reports that Rupert Murdock's journalists illegally hacked phones, Bushell contends that Murdock is up to push for the monopoly on news (Sabbagh, 2018). The Federal Communication Commission, according to the presenter, has allowed Murdoch to own various types of media in the same communities and thus control how Americans see the world. 'Murdoch's friends in power try to complete his grip' on all US press whilst the current media control already diverts Americans' attention away from the news that should most concern them (The Truthseeker, 2016n).

Where is Russia?

The most pronounced criticism of the 'crooked media' surfaces in episodes covering Russia-related news. However, RT also addresses the US domestic agenda, depicting evil government policies and the biases of the media against tackling what really bothers ordinary Americans. Some guests refer to RT as the only source of independent information in the country that challenges the monopoly of the 'mainstream media'. Episode 22 tells the story of the dead bees that have allegedly been poisoned by corporate chemicals in Florida – a fact the mainstream media has allegedly covered up. The host interviewed Anthony Gucciardi, a journalist, who contended that even though these US corporate crimes could have led to World War 3 and caused a massive economic collapse, it is left to states outside of the US to report upon the truth of the situation (The Truthseeker, 2016p). This implicit reference to the work RT does to uncover un-American plots is key in understanding the role that Russia is positioned to play in that context.

Along the lines of Surkov's ideological framework outlined in the previous chapter, Russia is depicted as the only power able to illuminate the atrocities that US-led powers commit across the world. Yet, the careful analysis of *The Truthseeker* reveals that Russia's presence in coverage of the events in the US is implicit. Presenters may rant for hours about the US government, the corporate media and big business, yet, the choice of speakers and topics from domestic and foreign policies do not point towards Russia as a beneficiary of this news. It is only when something big happens in Russia or a Russia-related sphere of politics, that *The Truthseeker* overtly positions itself as Russia's defence shield.

For instance, over the period of the 2014 Sochi Olympic Games, which were broadcast internationally by RT, significant international media attention was paid to the anti-LGBT laws recently passed by the Russian government (Friedman, 2014). *The Truthseeker*'s response was to deflect attention from Russia's internal problems by alleging a conspiracy of the mainstream media to silence reports of homophobia at home, whilst repeatedly soliciting criticisms of Russia's allegedly anti-gay environment from local LGBT activists (The Truthseeker, 2016q).

In a more bizarre way, *The Truthseeker* engaged with far-right American conspiracy theories when a terrorist attack was committed during the Boston marathon in April 2013 by two men of Chechen origin. In the emergency situation in Massachusetts that followed, the government used the national guard to search for the fugitives. At the same time, the posse comitatus law – which allows US citizens to create armed groups to protect themselves – was temporarily suspended. In discussing these developments, Bushell reproduced conspiracy theories of the posse comitatus movement of the US far right, which claim that the government seeks to strip US patriots of the power to protect themselves (The Truthseeker, 2016r). This movement lies behind the formation of militias in the second half of the 20th century, and has a history of both anti-Semitism and violent conflict with law-enforcement services (Corcoran, 1990). One of Bushell's guests, Kevin Barrett, explained that the 'rulers of America' use the media to create situations where US citizens would get involved in conflicts with each other. The US establishment, according to Barrett, creates conflicts – such as terrorist attacks – and uses them as a pretext to strip Americans of their rights. Straight after these words, Bushell anxiously notes that for the first time in history

> the Pentagon suspended the posse comitatus law that banned federal government from using the military for domestic policies. 'Tanks for the first time on the streets of America, Black hawks with laser-guided missiles on lawns, citizens forced out of their homes by soldiers.
>
> (The Truthseeker, 2016r)

The creators of *The Truthseeker* depicted the Boston attack as a classic US intelligence false flag operation of the US government aimed at curtailing the rights of US citizens and moreover, serving as a pretext to invade the Chechen republic. The focus on the false flag operations is a particular element of RT's agenda and extremely helpful in providing additional legitimacy to conspiratorial notions. For RT's presenters, the recorded false flag operations of the past serve as an important evidence of the US government's historic crimes. This reinforces the narrative that the allegations of RT's guests are historically founded, not necessarily paranoid.

The false flag operations of the US government in the past are used by *The Truthseeker* as the basis to claim that what happens in Syria, Iraq and Ukraine nowadays is also a false flag operation. The blatantly pro-Russian approach of RT has been illustrated by how *The Truthseeker*'s producers constructed the narrative of the programmes during the Ukraine crisis 2014–2015. Starting from episode 31, in which Bushell accused the CIA of attempting regime change, *The Truthseeker* devoted in total seven episodes to the situation in Ukraine. The overarching argument was that the US government has a long history of government overthrows and has an elaborate set of instruments to sow chaos and violence in countries that resist Washington's global agenda (The Truthseeker, 2016s). Bushell draws a shocking picture of NGOs, intelligence services and mainstream media working hand in hand to promote US interests across the world.

All pro-Ukrainian news in the global media are portrayed as 'US State Department created hoaxes', produced to make a path to power for US-backed fascists (The Truthseeker, 2016t). The presenter leaves no room for doubt that it was the US that stirred the conflict and provoked violent clashes to force Yanukovich to flee the country. The reasons for the plot are manifold: from expanding the area of US control to the pro-Russian state, to increasing public support of the country's leaders (The Truthseeker, 2016a). The historical links to the relations between US banks and the Nazi government also help *The Truthseeker* to extend the argument and claim that NATO supports neo-Nazis in Ukraine to wipe out any pro-Russian opposition (The Truthseeker, 2016u). Moreover, the final episode of the show aired before its cancellation was titled as brutally as possible: 'Genocide in Ukraine' (The Truthseeker, 2016v).

Jesse Ventura uncovers it all!

In July 2014 RT took *The Truthseeker* off the air following intense regulatory scrutiny, but in 2017 its niche was filled by another show: *The World According to Jesse*. Formerly a marine, WWF wrestler, governor of Minnesota and host of *Conspiracy Theory* on TruTV, presenter Jesse Ventura had previously accused the US government of conspiracies on several RT programmes.

Ventura's show more subtly repeats the narratives of *The Truthseeker*. Keeping the main subjects of conspiratorial criticism – big business, corrupt and imperialist government and crooked mainstream media – Ventura sets the scene of the show as a conversation about the corrupt US political system and constant governmental cover-ups.

Ventura's notable standing in US conspiracy culture, thanks to his previous show, is a great way of bringing this culture and the audience of his show to RT. One of the first episodes was devoted to the declassified documents in the JFK case – another major conspiracy theory, and cornerstone of US conspiracy culture. Ventura's approach describes JFK as a man who wanted to end the Cold War, but the global military-industrial complex together with the mob removed him and later removed Nikita Khrushchev, as both leaders were against large military spending (The World According to Jesse, 2017a). The show's guest, co-founder of the 'Coalition on political assassinations', insisted that the lack of some documents in the declassified files suggests that Trump was 'intimidated' by the same people who killed JFK.

The pragmatic usage of conspiracy theories by Ventura is evident from the way he engages with more extravagant conspiracy theories about aliens. The take on the alien conspiracy theories is again an anti-elitist one: according to Ventura and his guests the government keeps extra-terrestrial technologies secret because these would destroy the oil and gas business and power of the corporations (The World According to Jesse, 2018a). The same idea that politics is controlled by a small and secret cabal of power brokers, Ventura's show depicts the US president as unaware of the secret programmes. He basically refers to the idea of the Deep State – the bureaucracy that wields real power in the country and whose main principle is keeping secrets from those unaware of the real mechanisms of running the country.

On most of the topics picked up by producers of the show Ventura is able to provide a personal perspective – Ventura's multiple occupations in the past allow him to speak as an expert, what Joe Kennedy described as *authentocracy*, the tactic to wield power by referring to an authenticity (Kennedy, 2018). The starting point of discussions about the US military is Ventura's six-year-long service as a marine in Vietnam. Ventura speaks as a soldier and a patriot of the country who served in the war and who is against the government sending young soldiers to die. He continues talking about the large and unofficial military spending of the US addressing 'the common folk' assumed to watch the show, repeating ideas that the US army only drafts poor, middle class and black Americans, whilst 'rich boys' always stay at home (The World According to Jesse, 2017b). The populist criticism of the elite is thus clear and potentially appealing to large groups of the population.

Social problems, such as poor environment and health problems, are a good cause for Ventura to demonstrate his governmental experience as the governor of Minnesota. This former status is repeatedly highlighted by the show's producer Brigida Santos in her address to the presenter: 'Governor'. Ventura's status presents the possibility of the fair and good politician who can be trusted by people if he/she keeps distance from big corporations and crooked media (The World According to Jesse, 2017c).

Similar to *The Truthseeker*, Ventura lambasts the media that 'are controlled by the people on whom they must keep their eyes' (The World According to Jesse, 2017d). RT's show is thus presented as an opportunity for Ventura to speak freely in a country where big business and the government are in control of the media (The World According to Jesse, 2017e). 'RT never tells me what to do' screams Ventura, and argues that Americans are duped by the corporate media who realise the secret plan to keep US citizens 'in dark' and thus under control (The World According to Jesse, 2017f). By skilfully presenting investigative reporting of genuine CIA clandestine operations (Bernstein, 2007), Ventura extends these studies to the whole media landscape by arguing that the US media are in control of US intelligence (The World According to Jesse, 2018b).

This conspiratorial picture serves as a great way of channelling anti-US attitudes in the midst of the biggest US-Russia scandal over the alleged Putin-Trump collusion. The very first episode is devoted to Ventura's criticism of the US-Russia collusion story, which he explains as a symptom of US elites' desire to increase military spending – which requires a bogeyman (The World According to Jesse, 2017e). The presenters allow for the fact of possible intrusion into the elections, but counterweigh it with statistics about US interventions in foreign elections. This line is then continued in several episodes where Ventura depicts Putin and Russia as the US's potential partners that 'cry out for friendship' (The World According to Jesse, 2017d). The accusations that Russian hackers and bots could be behind the Black Lives Matter campaign are laughed at by Ventura as a hypocritical way of remaining blind to the real socio-economic issues (The World According to Jesse, 2018c). Here, the history of false flag operations – such as COINTELPRO, a FBI-operated programme that surveilled various American political movements in the 1950s–1970s (Churchill and Wall, 1990) – helps Ventura articulate legitimate criticism of US intelligence operations. 'Every problem we have in America, we blame on Russians. Isn't that convenient?' (The World According to Jesse, 2018c).

The questionable actions of big business often serve for RT's presenters as a trigger for anti-US criticism and a way to show that the Russian government is at least no better. The news that Google corporation has developed a censored search engine for China caused

Ventura's criticism of the US media coverage of Russiagate (Sheehan, 2018). The main threat to the US, according to Ventura, is in the big businesses that control elections and politicians (The World According to Jesse, 2018d). The news that Russia-affiliated actors spent 100 thousand dollars on Facebook advertisements to influence the elections opens the way for the presenter to argue how far from ideal the US electoral system is (Shane and Goel, 2017). 'People who don't follow the Constitution, they want to take our country. It happens internally, not externally' (The World According to Jesse, 2018d).

Conclusion

Tech giants that spy on US citizens, big media corporations that hide the truth, food chains that poison Americans, banks that steal from the common people and never bear responsibility for their crimes. These topics are a necessary background to put in question US policies and, they provide a breeding ground for mistrust that helps promote anti-US conspiracy theories. By examining these two conspiracy-focussed RT shows we are able to see how the rich tradition of conspiracy mythmaking in the US supported the network's production of the shows. Both 'The Truthseeker' and 'The World According to Jesse' operate in an environment that is rich with conspiratorial content and speakers – both from the Left and from the Right of the political spectrum – eager to engage in the conversation that is aimed at criticising the US government policies or the corporate world.

RT's most overtly conspiratorial outputs are conditioned to some extent by the nature of concerns and priorities already existing within conspiratorial public discourse. It is also, however, responsive to the broader media, regulatory and political environment. This is evidenced by the evolution in the approach between *The Truthseeker* and *The World According to Jesse*, and also in the way in which both are able to put aside their core topics of concern when the evolving news agenda demands it. What is notable is that despite this responsiveness to the changing news issues of the day, core populist tropes about corrupt government, corporations and mainstream media recur. This recurrence of core themes in the face of a changing news agenda is particularly evident in times of significant political crisis, as the following chapters demonstrate.

Note

1 The very first episode, as well as several others, has been deleted both from RT's website and from other video platforms.

References

American Constitutional Society. (2019). 'Key Findings of the Mueller Report', *American Constitutional Society*. Available at: https://www. acslaw.org/projects/the-presidential-investigation-education-project/other-resources/key-findings-of-the-mueller-report/ (Accessed: 12 November 2020).

Barkun, M. (2003). *A Culture of Conspiracy: Apocalyptic Visions in Contemporary America*. Berkeley: University of California Press.

Bernstein, C. (2007). *The CIA and the Media*. Available at: http://www.carlbernstein.com/magazine_cia_and_media.php (Accessed: 15 November 2020).

Churchill, W. and Wall, J.V. (1990). *Agents of Repression: The FBI's Secret Wars against the Black Panther Party and the American Indian Movement*. Boston, MA: South End Press.

Corcoran, J. (1990). *Bitter Harvest: Gordon Kahl and the Rise of the Posse Comitatus in the Heartland*. Viking Press.

Crosthwaite P., Knight P. and Marsh N. (2014). *Show Me the Money: The Image of Finance, 1700 to the Present*. Manchester: University of Manchester Press.

Friedman, U. (2014). 'How Sochi Became the Gay Olympics', *The Atlantic*, 28 January [Online]. Available at: https://www.theatlantic.com/international/archive/2014/01/how-sochi-became-the-gay-olympics/283398/ (Accessed: 15 November 2020).

Giddens, A. (1991). *The Consequences of Modernity*. Cambridge: Polity Press.

Greenwald, G., MacAskill, E. and Poitras, L. (2013). 'Edward Snowden: The Whistleblower Behind the NSA Surveillance Revelations', *The Guardian*, 11 June [Online]. Available at: https://www.theguardian.com/world/2013/jun/09/edward-snowden-nsa-whistleblower-surveillance (Accessed: 12 November 2020).

Griffin, D.R. (2005). 'The 911 Commission Report: A 571-Page Lie', *911Truth. org*. Available at: https://911truth.org/911-commission-report-571-page-lie/ (Accessed: 12 November 2020).

Kay, J. (2011). *Among the Truthers: A Journey through America's Growing Conspiracist Underground*. London: Harper.

Keith, J. (1994). *Black Helicopters over America: Strikeforce for the New World Order*. Lilburn: IllumiNet Press.

Kennedy, J. (2018). *Authenticity: Culture, Politics and the New Seriousness*. London: Repeater.

Leslie, I. (2016). 'The Sugar Conspiracy', *The Guardian*, 7 April [Online]. Available at: https://www.theguardian.com/society/2016/apr/07/the-sugar-conspiracy-robert-lustig-john-yudkin (Accessed: 14 November 2020).

Lewis, J.E. (2008). *The Mammoth Book of Cover-Ups*. Robinson Publishing.

Merlan, A. (2013). 'Times Square Billboard Calls for 'Independent Investigation' of 9-11 – and the People Speak', *Village Voice*, 15 October [Online]. Available at: https://www.villagevoice.com/2013/10/15/times-square-billboard-calls-for-independent-investigation-of-9-11-and-the-people-speak/ (Accessed: 12 November 2020).

Muirhead R. and Rosenblum, N.L. (2016). 'Speaking Truth to Conspiracy: Partisanship and Trust', *Critical Review*, 28(1), pp. 63–88.

Nelson, L. (2012). 'Farah: If Obama Re-elected, "We Will Be Hunted Down Like Dogs"', *Southern Poverty Law Center*, 9 July [Online]. Available at: https://www.splcenter.org/hatewatch/2012/07/09/farah-if-obama-re-elected-%E2%80%98we-will-be-hunted-down-dogs%E2%80%99 (Accessed: 20 November 2020).

Norwood, F.B., Calvo-Lorenzo, M.S., Lancaster, S. and Oltenacu, P.A. (2014) *Agricultural and Food Controversies: What Everyone Needs to Know*. Oxford: Oxford University Press.

Ofcom (2014). *Ofcom Broadcast Bulletin*. *Issue 288*. Available at: https://www.ofcom.org.uk/__data/assets/pdf_file/0017/50507/issue_288.pdf (Accessed 15 November 2020).

Raab, M.H., Carbon, C.C. and Ortlieb, S.A. (2013). 'Thirty Shades of Truth: Conspiracy Theories as Stories of Individuation, not of Pathological Delusion', *Frontiers in Psychology*. doi:10.3389/fpsyg.2013.00406.

Rae, D. (2014). *Big Pharma, Big Agri, Big Conspiracy: A New World Order on Drugs and GMO*. CreateSpace Independent Publishing Platform.

Sabbagh, D. (2018). 'Phone-hacking Cases against Murdoch Papers Settled at Last Minute', *The Guardian*, 18 January [Online]. Available at: https://www.theguardian.com/media/2018/jan/18/phone-hacking-cases-against-murdoch-papers-settled-at-last-minute (Accessed: 15 November 2020).

Sanders, T. and West, H. (2003). *Transparency and Conspiracy. Ethnographies of Suspicion in the New World Order*. Durham, NC: Duke University Press.

Schwartz, M. (2018). 'Who Killed the Kiev Protesters? A 3-D Model Holds the Clues', *The New York Times*, 30 May [Online]. Available at: https://www.nytimes.com/2018/05/30/magazine/ukraine-protest-video.html (Accessed: 13 November 2020).

Shane, S. and Goel, V. (2017). 'Fake Russian Facebook Accounts Bought $100,000 in Political Ads', *The New York Times*, 6 September [Online]. Available at: https://www.nytimes.com/2017/09/06/technology/facebook-russian-political-ads.html (Accessed: 15 November 2020).

Sheehan, M. (2018). 'How Google Took on China – and Lost', *MIT Technology Review*, 19 December [Online]. Available at: https://www.technology review.com/s/612601/how-google-took-on-china-and-lost/ (Accessed: 15 November 2020).

Sorkin, A.R. (2010). *Too Big To Fail: The Inside Story of How Wall Street and Washington Fought to Save the Financial System--and Themselves*. New York: Penguin Books.

Steele, A. (2013). '9/11 Free Fall: Richard Gage, Bob McIlvaine, and Deborah Voorhees Respond to Rachel Maddow', *911Blogger*, 3 May [Online]. Available at: http://911blogger.com/news/2013-05-03/911-free-fall-richard-gage-bob-mcilvaine-and-deborah-voorhees-respond-rachel-maddow-0 (Accessed: 13 November 2020).

The Truthseeker. (2016a). *E36 – Media 'staged' Syria Chem Attack* [YouTube]. Available at: https://youtu.be/f72Wxd7C5zw (Accessed: 13 November 2020).

The Truthseeker. (2016b). *E02 –Will America Kill?* [YouTube]. Available at: https://youtu.be/63YT07okMZg (Accessed: 14 November 2020).

The Truthseeker. (2016c). *E08 –You're Being Watched Now* [YouTube]. Available at: https://youtu.be/1fWmv9pHBTk (Accessed: 14 November 2020).

The Truthseeker. (2016d). *E18 – Obama's Arrest, Bush's Trial* [YouTube]. Available at: https://youtu.be/eE4sGq7mANg (Accessed: 20 November 2020).

The Truthseeker. (2016e). *E07 – We Came, We Saw, He Died* [YouTube]. Available at: https://youtu.be/n1JfdzliQQs (Accessed: 20 November 2020).

The Truthseeker. (2016f). *E11 – 3 War Tricks* [YouTube]. Available at: https://youtu.be/d5enSuaZKjQ (Accessed: 17 November 2020).

The Truthseeker. (2016g). *E16 –Manning Nobel Peace Prize Nomination* [YouTube]. Available at: https://youtu.be/iwjNLoFrYgY (Accessed: 18 November 2020).

The Truthseeker. (2016h). *E20 – America's Next Colonies Part 1.* Available at: https://youtu.be/1Obg7Fgzlic (Accessed: 17 November 2020).

The Truthseeker. (2016i). *E1 – Bribing Mr.Pre$ident* [YouTube]. Available at: https://youtu.be/BDxN5KwzZpg (Accessed: 16 November 2020).

The Truthseeker. (2016j). *E05–12Banks of Death* [YouTube]. Available at: https://youtu.be/unHYHorCOyA (Accessed: 16 November 2020).

The Truthseeker. (2016k). *E03 – McMuck* [YouTube]. Available at: https://youtu.be/Q-18BAgM9B0 (Accessed: 14 November 2020).

The Truthseeker. (2016l). *E29 – America 'Dead Last' in Education* [YouTube]. Available at: https://youtu.be/R7o1-NarUFk (Accessed: 14 November 2020).

The Truthseeker. (2016m). *E06 – Schools, Guns and Drugs* [YouTube]. Available at: https://youtu.be/gWCsp0irdDk (Accessed: 14 November 2020).

The Truthseeker. (2016n). *E10 – Presstitutes* [YouTube]. Available at: https://youtu.be/t0eoDeionEI (Accessed: 15 November 2020).

The Truthseeker. (2016o). *E36 – Media 'Staged' Syria Chem Attack* [YouTube]. Available at: https://youtu.be/f72Wxd7C5zw (Accessed: 15 November 2020).

The Truthseeker. (2016p). *E22 – US Civil War Is Coming* [YouTube]. Available at: https://youtu.be/ASQcEgnZ8xo (Accessed: 15 November 2020).

The Truthseeker. (2016q). *E34 –'Bag a Fg' a Silent US anti Gay Campaign* [YouTube]. Available at: https://youtu.be/zEnO-ISBwxw (Accessed: 15 November 2020).

The Truthseeker. (2016r). *E14 –Boston Bombing What You Aren't Told* [YouTube]. Available at: https://youtu.be/HQkcS9g8N_w (Accessed: 15 November 2020).

The Truthseeker. (2016s). *E31 –Leaked US Regime Change Manual, Admits Ukraine's Its 'Playbook'* [YouTube]. Available at: https://youtu.be/bBT0Wd edqpE (Accessed: 15 November 2020).

The Truthseeker. (2016t). *E35 –NGO Documents Plan Ukraine War* [YouTube]. Available at: https://youtu.be/aDrK3qb5xek (Accessed: 15 November 2020).

The Truthseeker. (2016u). *E41 –Neo Nazis NATO's Gladio Army in Ukraine* [YouTube]. Available at: https://youtu.be/YQ3jQR8C-dQ (Accessed: 15 November 2020).

The Truthseeker. (2016v). *E43 –Genocide of Eastern Ukraine (Last Episode)* [YouTube]. Available at: https://youtu.be/FfV_LzQv6e8 (Accessed: 15 November 2020).

The World According to Jesse. (2017a). RT, 18 November [Online]. Available at: https://www.rt.com/shows/the-world-according-to-jesse/410251-john-kennedy-jr-murdered/ (Accessed: 15 November 2020).

The World According to Jesse. (2017b). RT, 11 November [Online]. Available at: https://www.rt.com/shows/the-world-according-to-jesse/409545-vietnam-veterans-day-history/ (Accessed: 15 November 2020).

The World According to Jesse. (2017c). RT, 23 September [Online]. Available at: https://www.rt.com/shows/the-world-according-to-jesse/404323-big-pharma-issue-america/ (Accessed: 15 November 2020).

The World According to Jesse. (2017d). RT, 2 December [Online]. Available at: https://www.rt.com/shows/the-world-according-to-jesse/411705-john-kiriakou-threat-creation/ (Accessed: 15 November 2020).

The World According to Jesse. (2017e). RT, 11 September [Online]. Available at: https://www.rt.com/shows/the-world-according-to-jesse/402942-us-election-misconduct-media/ (Accessed: 15 November 2020).

The World According to Jesse. (2017f). RT, 16 December [Online]. Available at: https://www.rt.com/shows/the-world-according-to-jesse/413392-fcc-media-net-neutrality/ (Accessed: 15 November 2020).

The World According to Jesse. (2018a). RT, 28 January [Online]. Available at: https://www.rt.com/shows/the-world-according-to-jesse/417143-pentagon-ufo-secret-program/ (Accessed: 15 November 2020).

The World According to Jesse. (2018b). RT, 9 June [Online]. Available at: https://www.rt.com/shows/the-world-according-to-jesse/429221-operation-mockingbird-cia-surveillance/.

The World According to Jesse. (2018c). RT, 17 February [Online]. Available at: https://www.rt.com/shows/the-world-according-to-jesse/419093-black-press-fbi-program/

The World According to Jesse. (2018d). RT, 15 September. Available at: https://www.rt.com/shows/the-world-according-to-jesse/438519-government-censorship-social-media/ (Accessed: 15 November 2020).

Weir, L. (2008). 'The Concept of Truth Regime', *The Canadian Journal of Sociology / Cahiers Canadiens De Sociologie*, 33(2), pp. 367–389.

Yablokov, I. (2015). 'Conspiracy Theories as Russia's Public Diplomacy Tool: The Case of 'Russia Today (RT)', *Politics*, 35(3–4), pp. 301–315.

4 Conspiracy and democracy

Election meddling and #TrumpRussia

The 2016 Presidential elections in the US were beset with allegations of Russian meddling that subsequently evolved into a full-blown political scandal and the 2019 impeachment of the victor, President Donald Trump. Federal intelligence agencies rapidly investigated the allegations, and on 7 October 2016, the Department of Homeland Security (DHS) and Office of the Director of National Intelligence (ODNI) jointly stated that hacks directed from the highest levels of the Russian government were responsible for accessing the compromising emails from the Democratic National Committee (DNC) that had subsequently been released via WikiLeaks and DCLeaks. com (DHS, 2016). This operation, it was concluded, was 'consistent with the methods and motivations of Russian-directed efforts' (Hall Jamieson, 2018, p. 3).

By January 2017, the US Intelligence Agencies (CIA, FBI and NSA) jointly underlined their agreement that 'Putin and the Russian Government' attempted to influence the election (ODNI, 2017). The hacker, Guccifer 2.0, was exposed as a GRU (Russian military intelligence) front organisation. Later that year, Russia's international broadcasters, RT and Sputnik, were both obliged to register as foreign agents under the US FARA scheme (RFE/RL, 2018).

Public interest in the allegations continued throughout the subsequent investigation of Special Counsel Robert Mueller, which, in February 2018, resulted in the indictment of 13 Russians, allegedly responsible for electoral meddling via social media. The charges included 'conspiracy to defraud the United States', in order to subvert the lawful functioning of US political and electoral processes during the 2016 Presidential election, undermine public confidence in democracy and to favour the campaign of candidate Trump to the detriment of that of candidate Clinton (Hall Jamieson, 2018, pp. 4–5).

As Hall Jamieson noted in her 2018 examination of the meddling processes around the 2016 elections, the operations of the hackers and trolls involved were dependent on interactions between them: hackers linked to the Russian military intelligence stole compromising content and leaked it to actors including WikiLeaks for public dissemination. Bots then ensured that this content was amplified online, and went on to set agendas on online message boards and other social media platforms. These ultimately set the broader news agenda in battleground states (Hall Jamieson, 2018, pp. 6–7).

RT operates within this system. It is also implicated in the amplification of such stories leading-up to the 2016 Presidential elections, but also subsequently, in covering the ensuing scandal. This chapter examines how RT reported the Trump-Russia story across a variety of its outputs. Its main focus is on outputs giving in-depth analysis and engagement with stories being reported: two regular 30-minute discussion shows, and the website's op-ed section.

The first of the discussion programmes analysed is *CrossTalk* (CT), 'RT's flagship program', which appears intended for a broadly international audience and takes the form of an ostensible debate between two or three guests, moderated by a host, Peter Lavelle. The show does not subscribe to the standard conventions of a debate show, however, since the host does not act as an impartial Chair of the discussion. Instead, he takes up a significant proportion of airtime giving his own opinions on the topics discussed. Furthermore, in an average episode, guests tend to articulate a range of perspectives on the same general opinion orientation, rather than genuinely opposing views.

The second of the programmes is Watching the Hawks (WTH), aimed predominantly at a US audience, and focussed on issues within the US rather than globally. This being the case, even the coverage of the Russian meddling story is framed not so much about Russia as about the negative aspects of US domestic politics and the inadequacies of the mainstream media. In this series, a primary host, Tyrell Ventura (the son of Jesse Ventura), discusses 'media, politics and pop culture' with several other regular presenters and various guests.

Often the voices contributing to the Russiagate discussions appear to be pre-curated in ways that rendered their contributions somewhat more predictable. For instance, guests on both *Watching the Hawks* and *CrossTalk* included presenters of other RT shows, like Jesse Ventura and Alexey Yaroshevsky; or Sputnik employees like Lee Stranahan and Dmitri Babich. Both programmes also used a large number of 'network friends' as repeat guests: those who regularly contribute to RT or Sputnik. This trend was particularly pronounced on *CrossTalk*, where the same line-up of guests (Dmitri Babich, Mark Sleboda, Adam Garrie) was repeated with at most minor alterations, over the course of the Russiagate news cycle. Furthermore, almost every guest invited onto that programme over the period under analysis was male. The closeness of the guests to the network is, in some cases, presented as a factor that should boost their credibility with audiences. As *Cross-Talk*'s host, Peter Lavelle, states: 'I know you know something… and I agree with you because you've been on the programme before' (Cross-Talk, 2017a).

RT's reporting of the Trump-Russia meddling story emphasised five key tropes that undermined the allegations: (a) the 'establishment' actors making the allegations could not be trusted; (b) there were ulterior motives for blaming Russia; (c) there was no good evidence to substantiate the allegations against Russia; (d) the key accusations levelled at Russia actually applied to the US and finally, (e) that genuine prior conspiracies provided evidence that the latest allegations were themselves part of a conspiracy. These assertions undermined allegations of Russia's involvement, even as they were being reported.

You can't trust the establishment

RT consistently claimed that only corrupt representatives of the establishment accused Russia of meddling in the 2016. Presenters suggest that the CIA's claims cannot be trusted due to its own historical overseas meddling, and that PR companies and the Democrat party have boosted the agency's Russian meddling narrative for their own purposes (Watching the Hawks, 2016a). Hosts and commentators question whether the intelligence community has real evidence for its allegations (CrossTalk, 2016a) and suggest that the CIA is suspiciously close to the media (RT, 2016a). RT also uses its well-honed tactic of using mocking dismissals to avoid dealing substantively with uncomfortable allegations (Crilley and Chatterje-Doody, 2020; Tolz et al., 2020). There are mocking comments about RT itself being a threat to US democracy (Watching the Hawks, 2017a), and about a Russian 'bogeyman' (CrossTalk, 2017b, 2017o) being used to hide the divisiveness of Hillary Clinton's own candidacy. In various cases, mocking of supposedly hysterical attitudes to Russia was repurposed as Twitter content.[1]

The intelligence agencies responsible for making allegations of Russian meddling in the election are presented as unreliable, staffed with enemies of President Trump (CrossTalk, 2016a, 2017c) and politicised and/or untrustworthy (CrossTalk, 2017n). They are also portrayed as supportive of radicals including ISIS, in the Middle East (CrossTalk,

2017d), a practice that it is indicated Trump would resist (CrossTalk, 2017e). In Watching the Hawks (2017b) the hosts allege that the FBI is not checking the available evidence surrounding claims that Ukraine was ultimately implicated in the hacking of the DNC, and a guest explains this in terms of a high-level conspiracy involving a cyber security company, intelligence agencies and a leading think tank. In this most explicit example of conspiracy theorising on this show, the conspiracy theory is articulated not by one of the hosts, but by the guest, Alexey Yaroshevsky. However, this guest is himself a staff member of RT.

The political and professional reliability of the intelligence agencies is consistently called into question over the evolution of the Trump-Russia story. It is alleged that the NSA is itself not confident in the conclusion of Russian hacking, and that the FBI cannot be trusted (CrossTalk, 2017e). The intelligence services are portrayed as politically subservient to an Obama White House, producing reports to political orders (CrossTalk, 2017f), or as being in league with the DNC (CrossTalk, 2017g). At the very least, the intelligence services are portrayed as being out of control over the alleged wiretapping of Trump. At the worst, the intelligence agencies are alleged by the host of seeking to prematurely end Trump's Presidency (CrossTalk, 2017c). Indeed, several programmes suggest that the investigators should themselves be investigated (CrossTalk, 2017g, 2017n).

Political parties, and the Democratic party in particular, are portrayed as hostages to their powerful corporate backers, including Saudi financiers, the 'media-industrial complex' and the 'military-industrial complex' (CrossTalk, 2016b, 2017e). Indeed, this line about a fundamentally corrupt Democratic party is rearticulated in the 2020 US presidential campaign, with mocking Tweets noting Clinton's renewed accusations of meddling 'because it worked so well in 2016';[2] reporters making equivalent claims are similarly mocked.[3]

Similar arguments are applied after the publication of the Mueller report. It is painted as propaganda exercise to support a CIA psychological operation to oblige Trump to keep forces in the Middle East (Watching the Hawks, 2018). Non-governmental organisations are also treated with scepticism, as powerful actors pursuing their own agenda (CrossTalk, 2017h), and as unaccountable, politically partisan bodies that meddle in the affairs of other states, such as Ukraine (CrossTalk, 2017p).

The mainstream media's reporting of the meddling saga is frequently drawn into question (CrossTalk, 2017i). As well as outright accusations of corporate corruption and disinterest in truthful reporting (CrossTalk, 2017c), the 'fail stream media' is accused of dehumanising behaviour towards Russia, as well as a tendency to throw accusations at RT itself (Watching the Hawks, 2017c). The mainstream media is also portrayed as having a blatant preference for Clinton (CrossTalk, 2016c) and – in conjunction with the Democrat party – treating media consumers as idiots who will believe whatever they are told, regardless of evidence (Watching the Hawks, 2017d). In some cases, it is alleged outright that mainstream media outlets like MSNBC may be working for government agencies like the Pentagon or CIA (Watching the Hawks, 2017e), and that mainstream media deliberately plants false stories with approval (Watching the Hawks, 2017f). The power of the mainstream supposedly dwarfs any meddling potential Russia could have. In such an environment, it is DC policymakers that remain under-informed, according to RT. They are locked within a neo-Conservative echo chamber that makes any idea of rapprochement with Russia unthinkable. This, the host suggests, is because stereotypes, not facts, influence policymakers (CrossTalk, 2016d).

Ulterior motives

One of the recurring themes in RT's coverage of the meddling saga was that the allegations were motivated by Russophobia, which is a recurring theme on RT, evoked by hosts and guests alike. Guests represent Russophobia as a tale as old as time (CrossTalk, 2017l); liken it to the 20th-century scapegoating of Jews (CrossTalk, 2016e) and draw historical parallels to McCarthyism (CrossTalk, 2017k). An entire episode of Watching the Hawks (2017i) is dedicated to discussion of a book by Dan Kovalik, which interrogates a historical tradition of demonising Russia in order to justify US invasion. Using the supposedly historical context of Russophobia, the hosts advocate close scrutiny of the intelligence agencies' narratives of Russian meddling given historical provocations of the US government and CIA overseas.

This leads into RT's claims that Russophobia is being employed for practical aims: to boost the economic interests of the military-industrial complex (CrossTalk, 2017h; Watching the Hawks, 2017j); to neutralise Russian competition in the cyber security industry (Watching the Hawks, 2017k); to squeeze RT out of the mediaspace (Cross-Talk, 2016a); to distract from politicians' own failings (CrossTalk 2017n), or from serious domestic issues (CrossTalk, 2017l); to allow the deep state to impose tyranny in the US (Watching the Hawks, 2017l) and to resist Russia's obstruction of globalist ideology (CrossTalk, 2017k). In this regard, the Democratic party, and Hillary Clinton personally, are portrayed as terroristic puppet masters (CrossTalk, 2017m) leaking information to support a narrative of Russian hackers to support their own political ends.

Even under Trump, the White House is portrayed as conspiring against the President to damage relations with Russia (CrossTalk, 2017i) and the theme of a 'deep state' anti-Trump coup plot between intelligence agencies and liberal media organisations often comes up (CrossTalk, 2017d; see also CrossTalk, 2016a). Indeed, President Putin himself made a similar claim in some detail, drawing parallels to his own interpretation of a manufactured Maidan protest (Machon, 2016; RT, 2017). This coverage therefore replicates narratives favoured both by the Russian side and by Trump that the deep state is seeking to undermine and depose him, including his claims about wiretapping under the Obama administration (Baker et al, 2019; CrossTalk, 2017b). Indeed one of CrossTalk's chyrons states explicitly: 'Critics: political elites intend to cripple Trump, plan impeachment' (CrossTalk, 2017c), and one guest suggests that the intelligence agencies' interest in possible collusion is a direct response to Trump's willingness to talk openly about the operations of the 'deep state' (CrossTalk, 2017j).

This 'deep state' conspiracy theory idea had been used throughout the 20th century in Turkey to delegitimise political opponents (Nefes, 2018), and spread rapidly throughout US politics in the 2010s, where it was used by the conservatives and the far-right to accuse opponents of destroying America from inside. Donald Trump, and his former ideological aide Steven Bannon, were central in spreading these conspiracies across society (Rohde, 2020). RT's appropriation of Trump's 'deep state' conspiracy language to defend Russia's international position illustrates the globality of conspiracy cultures in the 21st century and the rapidity with which RT's staff reacts to emerging issues. Its discussions of the 'deep state' insinuated that the concept had gone from being thought of in the realm of conspiracy theories, to an accepted phenomenon whose extent and implications were being analysed and measured (CrossTalk, 2017h).

Actors as varied as the Henry Jackson society and the businessman Jeff Bezos are identified as having links to the 'deep state' (CrossTalk, 2017c). In a telling moment, when one guest, Matthew Sheffield, disputes that the work of an elite conspiracy is at play, the show's host immediately breaks the air for a commercial break (CrossTalk, 2017h). Following the break, the discussion continues under the chyron 'Trending: observers concerned intel agencies become overly politicised'. Here, discussion ranges from one guest's explicitly conspiratorial rendering of a US deep state and global conspiracy, visually endorsed by the host's nodding, to the more sceptical guest's carefully chosen words interpreting the deep state primarily as the unelected people who shape policies behind the scenes (CrossTalk, 2017h). This particular theme is the dominant one on *CrossTalk*'s coverage for approximately three weeks from 17 March 2017, when almost every show is about Russiagate and all the stories relate to Trump vs Deep State.

Where's the evidence?

RT reported several angles on a popular conspiracy theory that the DNC emails were not leaked, but hacked by a concerned insider. Beginning on pro-Trump message boards, these theories gained traction when high profile political and media commentators amplified them, and when WikiLeaks offered a substantial reward for information leading to the conviction of the killer of a DNC staffer falsely identified as the source (Hall Jamieson, 2018, p. 25). In some cases, the wording of RT's Chyrons insinuated that the 'leak' was fact rather than theory: 'Critics: Clinton, DNC, Podesta not hacked. Source was internal leak'; 'Foreign policy establishment & top members of GOP against better ties' (CrossTalk, 2016e). In its web reporting, RT amplified former intelligence whistle-blowers' claims that no genuine hack could have occurred undetected by the NSA (RT, 2016b). One of the claimants (formerly of the CIA, and an RT network regular, Ray McGovern) appeared the following day on *CrossTalk* repeating the same argument. Other guests and the hosts allege that someone inside the 'establishment' produced the Russia hack story and that it formed part of a conspiracy between the CIA and mainstream media to subvert the constitutional order, delegitimise Trump and undermine the will of voters (CrossTalk, 2017f). The same day, a second online report appeared on RT with the same allegation, this time attributed to a 'WikiLeaks envoy', a former UK Ambassador-turned whistle-blower and RT regular, Craig Murray (RT, 2016c).

A later *CrossTalk* guest (on a programme in which McGovern also appears) doubted the NSA's confidence in the conclusion of Russian hacking (CrossTalk, 2017e). The same cycle of guests repeatedly raised issues with the forensic evidence for an external hack, citing disparities in time stamp data and suggesting that the story was more likely a deliberate distraction from scandals internal to the Democratic party (CrossTalk, 2017f; Watching the Hawks, 2017m, 2017o). The falsification of this time stamp evidence by Guccifer 2.0, and the identity of Guccifer 2.0 as a GRU front were subsequently clearly established (Campbell, 2018), but some two years later, RT was still repurposing and pushing as Tweets packages that disputed the forensic evidence.[4]

Indeed, RT's standard line is to emphasise a lack of evidence for allegations in its serial reporting. So, an RT News segment (RT News, 2016) dedicated to anticipated US retaliatory sanctions for Russian election meddling presents a montage of US media referring to 'hacking' and 'meddling', with RT's anchor's own commentary consistently noting that these actions are merely 'alleged', and that 'no concrete proof has been presented on Moscow's involvement'. This idea frequently recurs that intelligence agencies and mainstream media have made allegations without evidence (CrossTalk, 2017b, 2017i), and contrasts with RT's willingness to suggest, without evidence, that the DNC or other powers more likely guilty of collusion, or at least of conspiracy against Trump (CrossTalk, 2017a, 2017n). It is a guest's assertion of this nature, that prompts a comment from the host that sums up the whole approach of *CrossTalk* to what counts as reliable evidence: 'I know you know something, and I agree with you because you've been on this programme before' (CrossTalk, 2017a).

RT often used humour to rebut the most outlandish allegations against Russia, insinuating that all allegations were equally implausible. For instance, episodes of Watching the Hawks on 9 and 14 September 2017 present the Washington Post's suggestions that Russia may have poisoned Hillary Clinton as a laughable testament to the inadequacy of the mainstream media (Watching the Hawks, 2016b, 2016c). Dmitry Babich, a Sputnik employee and frequent *CrossTalk* guest, jokes about how surprising it is that Hillary Clinton has not accused Russia of driving immigrants into the US (CrossTalk, 2017m). An entire episode of *CrossTalk* (CrossTalk, 2017o), 'Evidence-free' questions the evidence for various types of allegation against Russia, with one guest dismissing the documented Russian troll factories as an invented image. Similarly, one *CrossTalk* guest objects to the WikiLeaks releases being reported alongside news of Russian hacking, as this suggests that they were connected (CrossTalk, 2016b).

The substance of the intelligence agencies' findings is represented by one guest as 'opinions' that should be fact-checked (CrossTalk, 2016c), given the notion that their activities are politicised (CrossTalk, 2017j). When RT News broke the news of the post-Muller report indictment of Russian nationals for election meddling, it stressed the conclusions that their 'supposed actions actually had no impact on the outcome' (RT News, 2018a,c). Together with the continual questioning of the evidence base for meddling allegations, RT's coverage suggests that the general public does not believe in the allegations against Russia (Watching the Hawks, 2018b).

The US is the guilty party, not Russia!

One of RT's consistently favoured themes is that of Western hypocrisy, and its Russiagate coverage made clear the US democracy was already fundamentally defective. It is not the people, but corporations, PR companies, intelligence organisations and government departments that run US politics (Watching the Hawks, 2016b, 2016d, 2016e, 2016f). In its most developed form, the narrative implies that the US is no more than a two-party dictatorship (Watching the Hawks, 2017e).

RT's coverage also mirrors or deflects many of the specific accusations levelled at Russia. At some times, RT has presented the real 'meddling threat' as coming not from Russia, but from China – as when its Twitter feed amplified Vice President Mike Pence's claims to this effect.[5] At other times, domestic forces are portrayed as the real source of meddling, whether this is the corrupt federal intelligence services (CrossTalk, 2016a) or the domestic mainstream media, that a Columbia University research report concludes were 'indirectly involved in meddling themselves' due to automated content amplification (RT News, 2018b). Allegations against Russia are thus presented as hypocritical: when the host of *CrossTalk* suggests that Clinton herself ran a 'troll factory' (CrossTalk, 2016a); when guests on *CrossTalk* (CrossTalk, 2017p) allege that a taxpayer-funded Orwellian surveillance state is monitoring media consumers' engagement with RT and Sputnik and when Watching the Hawks co-host Tabitha Wallace accuses CNN of producing conspiracy theories about a Kremlin-Trump campaign plot against it (Watching the Hawks, 2017n).

These mirroring and deflection techniques recurred throughout reporting of the Russiagate scandal. According to RT, the US, not Russia, is the real cyberwarfare aggressor: it blocked WikiLeaks to stop access to the DNC emails and to demonstrate its own cyberwarfare capacity to the Russian side (Watching the Hawks, 2016g); and it planned to conduct cyberwar against Russia in retaliation for 'unproven election meddling'.[6] The post-Muller report indictments were, in RT's telling, a 'case of pot calling the kettle black'.[7] Similarly, during the 2020 election campaign, when a draft report from the Department of Homeland Security alleged that Russia would raise questions about candidates' physical and mental fitness to meddle in those elections, RT News responded with a montage demonstrating how US mainstream television networks made precisely that kind of speculation (RT News, 2020).

Conspiracy reporting and the democratic process

RT's coverage of the allegations of Russian meddling in the US Presidential elections often amplified conspiratorial allegations that had come out of the Trump administration itself, and suggested that the 'establishment' actors making the allegations could not be trusted; there were ulterior motives for the allegations; the evidence for the allegations was missing or faulty or that the accusations levelled at Russia actually applied to the US. Historical examples were often cited as evidence that the contemporary allegations themselves formed part of a conspiracy. RT's News coverage of Russian meddling in the 2016 US Presidential elections emphasised that allegations being reported were unproven and frequently cited overblown US media reports as evidence that 'Russophobia' lay behind the allegations. What is more, where greater analysis of the Russiagate news item was offered, this selectively included reputable research that supported RT's line – as in the low overall impact of meddling activities, or the unknowing contribution of mainstream media to the process.

A 'parallel commentariat' of experts frequently found on RT and Sputnik, but who rarely feature on other international media (Ramsay and Robertshaw, 2018, p. 6) produced much of RT's analysis. Many of these are 'network friends' who contribute to both broadcasters as presenters, invited guests and by penning op-eds. This can be viewed as a form of pre-curation of the network's content, in as much as the perspectives and views of these guests are not only well-known, but reliably close to one another in perspective. Guests tended to provide variations on similar perspectives on the issues under discussion, rather than vastly diverging views. What is more, when genuine dissent appeared on discussion programmes, it was talked over or shut down.

In RT's conspiratorial reading of the Trump-Russia story, the main villains were not always clearly and consistently articulated but conformed to certain patterns. They included the members and structures of formally recognised institutions of social power, including the intelligence agencies, the DNC, the mainstream media, the military-industrial complex and the media-industrial complex. As these latter combined categories make clear, cooperation between the respective villains was generally implied, and in many cases this took the form of outright allegations against the 'deep state'. In questioning the trustworthiness of these key actors, it was implied that history showed how they had their own ulterior motives for levelling allegations at Russia – ranging from base Russophobia, through commercial motivations, to hopes for a full-blown anti-democratic coup. Where RT engaged directly with the concept of conspiracy theories, it was to accuse other parties, or to allege that once-dismissed theories had now become established facts that its coverage was analysing in detail. This probably accurately reflects the perspective of most of the pre-curated contributor pool, who tended to take for granted the conspiratorial framing through which the meddling allegations were reported.

As well as casting doubt on the legitimacy of all of the major sources of information about the progression of the Trump-Russia enquiry, RT's coverage called into question the evidence that these agencies and actors reported, and by extension, the facts of the case themselves. In such practices, the network was not acting alone, but rather was actively engaged with conspiracy theories already in circulation in the global media environment, whether these came from the Russian or American political elite; mainstream media commentators; or partisan online message boards.

RT served as one of the actors unapologetically operating in an online ecosystem which routinely undermines formerly reliable sources of information, as well as the specific facts that they report. In the wider context of the global media such practices call into question the basis for how we understand and accept what is fact – the nature of social knowledge itself. Furthermore, in calling into question established sources of legitimacy, whilst insinuating that expert analysis and minority-held opinions are no different from one another, conspiratorial coverage of the Trump-Russia phenomenon cast a long shadow. As the following chapter makes clear, many of these trends were reflected in reporting of the 2018 Skripal poisonings in the UK, and were later thrown into sharp relief during the subsequent COVID-19 pandemic – a topic that we return to in the concluding chapter.

Notes

1 @RT_com Tweet on meddling hysteria, November 6th, 2018, available at: https://twitter.com/RT_com/status/1059826490026553346. See also tweet of the asking 'How many Russian octopuses do you know?', September 4th, 2019, available at: https://twitter.com/rt_com/status/1169158154724216834

2 @RT_com, February 21st, 2020, available at: https://twitter.com/RT_com/status/1230962417200435200

3 @RT_com, August 10th, 2020, available at: https://twitter.com/RT_com/status/1292717315415515136

4 'No forensics. Why? There was no hacking in the first place: Fmr CIA officer on 'Russian meddling' @RT_com, 11th January, 2019, available at: https://twitter.com/RT_com/status/1083800717771575296

5 @RT_com Tweet, 4th October, 2018, available at: https://twitter.com/
RT_com/status/1047704401891287041
6 @RT_com, 29th December, 2019, available at: https://twitter.com/rt_com/
status/1211186144861446144
7 @RT_com, February 20th, 2018, available at: https://twitter.com/rt_com/
status/965876176899190785

References

Baker, P., Jakes, L., Barnes, J.E., LaFraniere, S., and Wong, E. (2019). 'Trump's War on the 'Deep State' Turns against Him', *The New York Times*, 23 October [Online]. Available at: https://www.nytimes.com/2019/10/23/us/politics/trump-deep-state-impeachment.html (Accessed: 16 December 2020).

Campbell, D. (2018). 'Briton Ran Pro-Kremlin Disinformation Campaign That Helped Trump Deny Russian Links', *Computerweekly.com*, 31 July [Online]. Available at: https://www.computerweekly.com/news/252445769/Briton-ran-pro-Kremlin-disinformation-campaign-that-helped-Trump-deny-Russian-links (Accessed: 16 November 2020).

Crilley, R. and Chatterje-Doody, P.N. (2020) 'From Russia with Lols: Humour, RT, and the Legitimation of Russian Foreign Policy', *Global Society*. Early View. doi:10.1080/13600826.2020.1839387

CrossTalk. (2016a) 'Bullhorns: Coup Attempt?', *RT*, 12 December [Online]. Available at: https://www.rt.com/shows/CrossTalk/369969-american-election-russian-influence/ (Accessed: 16 November 2020).

CrossTalk. (2016b) 'Bullhorns Electioneering!', *RT*, 7 November [Online]. Available at: https://www.rt.com/shows/CrossTalk/365577-close-us-presidential-elections/ (Accessed: 16 November 2020).

CrossTalk. (2016c). 'Mainstream's Revenge', *RT*, 14 December [Online]. Available at: https://www.rt.com/shows/CrossTalk/370221-mainstream-media-fight-control/ (Accessed: 16 November 2020).

CrossTalk. (2016d). 'Donald & Vladimir', *RT*, 18 November [Online]. Available at: https://www.rt.com/shows/CrossTalk/367359-trump-us-relations-russia/ (Accessed: 16 November 2020).

CrossTalk. (2016e). 'Bullhorns: Blaming Putin', *RT*, 19 December [Online]. Available at: https://www.rt.com/shows/CrossTalk/370704-western-elites-blame-russia/ (Accessed: 16 November 2020).

CrossTalk. (2017a). 'Who Really Colluded?', *RT*, 27 October [Online]. Available at: https://www.rt.com/shows/CrossTalk/407924-trump-russia-election-colluding/ (Accessed: 16 November 2020).

CrossTalk. (2017b). 'Russiagate', *RT*, 24 March [Online]. Available at: https://www.rt.com/shows/CrossTalk/382133-russia-influence-us-election/ (Accessed: 16 November 2020).

CrossTalk. (2017c). 'Unhinged Intel', *RT*, 5 April [Online]. Available at: https://www.rt.com/shows/CrossTalk/383541-russian-phantoms-obama-administration/ (Accessed: 16 November 2020).

CrossTalk. (2017d) 'Palace Coup?', *RT*, 17 February [Online]. Available at: https://www.rt.com/shows/CrossTalk/377675-flynn-us-security-politucs/ (Accessed: 16 November 2020).

CrossTalk. (2017e). 'Russia & Leaks', *RT*, 29 March [Online]. Available at: https://www.rt.com/shows/CrossTalk/382643-washington-politics-russialeaks/ (Accessed: 16 November 2020).

CrossTalk. (2017f). 'Russia Card', *RT*, 4 January [Online]. Available at: https://www.rt.com/shows/CrossTalk/370503-america-europe-politics-russia/ (Accessed: 16 November 2020).

CrossTalk. (2017g). 'Investigating Mueller', *RT*, 3 November [Online]. Available at: https://youtu.be/3HBKYAfNQZQ (Accessed: 16 November 2020).

CrossTalk. (2017h). 'Deep State', *RT*, 17 March [Online]. Available at: https://youtu.be/CZdOj34KRW4 (Accessed: 16 November 2020).

CrossTalk. (2017i). 'Targeting Russia', *RT*, 6 January [Online]. Available at: https://youtu.be/S1G94BcX5wo (Accessed: 16 November 2020).

CrossTalk. (2017j). 'Bullhorns: FBI-gate', *RT*, 18 December [Online]. Available at: https://youtu.be/4fHMb-siw90 (Accessed: 16 November 2020).

CrossTalk. (2017k). 'Bullhorns: Eavesdropping', *RT*, 3 April [Online]. Available at: https://www.rt.com/shows/CrossTalk/383172-russiagate-story-steameavesdropping/ (Accessed: 17 November 2020).

CrossTalk. (2017l). 'Imagining Russia', *RT*, 20 October [Online]. Available at: https://www.rt.com/shows/CrossTalk/407271-valdai-discussion-clubrussia/ (Accessed: 16 November 2020).

CrossTalk. (2017m). 'Bullhorns: On Offence', *RT*, 24 October [Online]. Available at: https://youtu.be/EIoNT43Fz98 (Accessed: 16 November 2020).

CrossTalk. (2017n). 'CrossTalk on Russia Probe: Collapsing Confidence', *RT*, 15 December [Online]. Available at: https://youtu.be/UxIz_bCdNuA (Accessed: 16 November 2020).

CrossTalk. (2017o). 'CrossTalk Bullhorns: Evidence-free?', *RT*, 2 October [Online]. Available at: https://youtu.be/4bDvqmy80vk (Accessed: 16 November 2020).

CrossTalk. (2017p). 'CrossTalk: Bullhorns: Targeting RT (EXTENDED VERSION)', *RT*, 7 August [Online]. Available at: https://youtu.be/ZJKkhQrjO88 (Accessed: 16 November 2020).

DHS. (2016, October 7). Joint Statement from the DHS and ODNI on Election Security. Available at: https://www.dhs.gov/news/2016/10/07/joint-statement-department-homeland-security-and-office-director-national.

Hall Jamieson, K. (2018). *Cyberwar: How Russian Hackers and Trolls Helped Elect a President. What We Don't Can't and Do Know.* New York: OUP.

Machon, A. (2016). 'Is the United States Facing a Coup d'etat?', *RT*, 18 December [Online]. Available at: https://www.rt.com/op-ed/370672-united-states-coup-trump-electoral-college/ (Accessed: 16 November 2020).

Nefes, T. (2018).'The Conspiratorial Style in Turkish Politics: Discussing the Deep State in the Parliament', in J. Uscinsky (ed.) *Conspiracy Theories and the People Who Believe Them.* New York: Oxford University Press, pp. 386–393.

ODNI. (2017, January 6). Background to 'Assessing Russian Activities and Intentions in Recent US Elections': The Analytic Process and Cyber Incident Attribution. Available at: https://www.dni.gov/files/documents/ICA_2017_01.pdf.

Ramsay, G. and Robertshaw, S. (2018). Weaponising News: RT, Sputnik and Targeted Disinformation. King's College London: The Policy Institute. Available at: https://www.kcl.ac.uk/policy-institute/assets/weaponising-news.pdf.

RFE/RL. (2018). 'Sputnik Partner 'Required to Register' under U.S. Foreign-Agent Law', *Radio Free Europe/Radio Liberty*, 10 January [Online]. Availableat:https://www.rferl.org/a/sputnik-partner-says-required-to-register-united-states-fara-law/28967234.html (Accessed: 16 November 2020).

Rohde, D. (2020). 'How America Escapes Its Conspiracy Theory Crisis', *The New Yorker*, 29 October [Online]. Available at: https://www.newyorker.com/news/the-future-of-democracy/how-america-escapes-its-conspiracy-theory-crisis (Accessed: 20 December 2020).

RT. (2016a). 'CIA Provides Info to Media but Not Congress' – Homeland Security Committee on Russia Hacking Claims', *RT*, 16 December [Online]. Available at: https://www.rt.com/usa/370569-cia-russia-congress-briefing/ (Accessed: 16 November 2020).

RT. (2016b). 'DNC Docs Were Leaked, Not Hacked, Intelligence Veterans Say', *RT*, 15 December [Online]. Available at: https://www.rt.com/usa/370447-russia-hack-intelligence-dissent/ (Accessed: 16 November 2020).

RT. (2016c). 'WikiLeaks Envoy: Leaked DNC Emails Came from 'Disgusted' Whistleblower, Not Russian Hackers', *RT*, 16 December [Online]. Available at: https://www.rt.com/news/370478-dnc-emails-whistleblower-russia/ (Accessed: 16 November 2020).

RT. (2017) "Worse Than Prostitutes': Putin Slams Those Behind Trump 'Leak'", *RT*, 17 January [Online]. Available at: https://www.rt.com/news/373951-putin-trump-attack-protect/ (Accessed: 17 November 2020).

RT News. (2016). *RT*. 29 December [Online] Available at: https://www.rt.com/shows/news/372132-rtnews-december-29-12msk/ (Accessed: 16 November 2020).

RT News. (2018a). *RT*. 17 February [Online]. Available at: https://www.rt.com/shows/news/419088-rtnews-february-17-12msk/ (Accessed: 17 November 2020).

RT News. (2018b). *RT*. 16 February [Online]. Available at: https://www.rt.com/shows/news/419025-rtnews-february-16-17msk/ (Accessed: 16 November 2020).

RT News. (2018c). *RT*. 9 August [Online]. Available at: https://www.rt.com/shows/news/435504-rtnews-august-09-12msk/ (Accessed: 16 November 2020).

RT News. (2020). *RT*. 4 September [Online]. Available at: https://www.rt.com/shows/news/499841-rtnews-september-04-12msk/ (Accessed: 16 November 2020).

Tolz, V., Hutchings, S., Chatterje-Doody, P.N., and Crilley, R. (2020). 'Mediatization and Journalistic Agency: Russian Television Coverage of the Skripal Poisonings', *Journalism*. Early View. doi:10.1177/14648849 20941967

Watching the Hawks. (2016a). 'A Hack of a Problem & 9/11 JASTA Justice', *RT*, 12 December [Online]. Available at: https://www.rt.com/shows/watching-the-hawks/370102-hack-problem-justice-us/ (Accessed: 16 November 2020).

Watching the Hawks. (2016b). 'The New McCarthyism & The Marijuana Manifesto w/ Jesse Ventura', *RT*, 9 September [Online]. Available at: https://youtu.be/p8otE2C_AUU (Accessed: 17 November 2020).

Watching the Hawks. (2016d). 'Fighting for Feminism: Taking on Privilege in America (E369)', *RT*, 3 December [Online]. Available at: https://www.rt.com/shows/watching-the-hawks/369085-rape-culture-burkini-ban/ (Accessed: 16 November 2020).

Watching the Hawks. (2016e). 'Watching the Hawks & the Fight for African-American Justice (E373)', *RT*, 9 December [Online]. Available at: https://www.rt.com/shows/watching-the-hawks/369731-fight-african-american-justice/ (Accessed: 16 November 2020).

Watching the Hawks. (2016f). 'The US Security State: Usurping Our Sovereign Power (E374)', *RT*, 10 December [Online]. Available at: https://www.rt.com/shows/watching-the-hawks/369862-us-security-state-nsa/ (Accessed: 16 November 2020).

Watching the Hawks. (2016g). 'DNC Hacked Reality & #FRAMEYemen (E319)', *RT*, 15 September [Online]. Available at: https://www.rt.com/shows/watching-the-hawks/359382-us-governors-yemen-war/ (Accessed: 16 November 2020).

Watching the Hawks. (2017a). 'Surreal New Cold War, and the Cyberwar against You (E391)', *RT*, 6 January [Online]. Available at: https://www.rt.com/shows/watching-the-hawks/372801-washington-post-fake-news/ (Accessed: 16 November 2020).

Watching the Hawks. (2017b). 'When Reform Becomes Surveillance and CrowdStrike's Out (E445)', *RT*, 24 March [Online]. Available at: https://www.rt.com/shows/watching-the-hawks/382126-russian-hacking-cybersecurity-us/ (Accessed: 17 November 2020).

Watching the Hawks. (2017c). 'Fail Stream Media w/Alexey Yaroshevsky', *RT*, 25 January [Online]. Available at: https://www.youtube.com/watch?v=f7sw_p9qpZw (Accessed: 16 November 2020).

Watching the Hawks. (2017d). 'Russia Blame Game & Palestine Joins IN-TERPOL (E573)', *RT*, 29 September [Online]. Available at: https://www.rt.com/shows/watching-the-hawks/404978-russian-election-facebook-interpol/ (Accessed: 16 November 2020).

Watching the Hawks. (2017e). 'Russiagate Takes Scalps & Debating Term Limits (E617)', *RT*, 2 December [Online]. Available at: https://www.rt.com/shows/watching-the-hawks/411708-michael-flynn-pleads-guilty/ (Accessed: 16 November 2020).

Watching the Hawks. (2017f). 'CNN: A Year in Lies (E622)', *RT*, 12 December [Online]. Available at: https://www.rt.com/shows/watching-the-hawks/412807-cnn-fake-news-terror/ (Accessed: 16 November 2020).

Watching the Hawks. (2017g). 'Donna Brazil Un-Hacks the Election', *RT*, 9 November [Online]. Available at: https://youtu.be/kwsvafUptcE (Accessed: 16 November 2020).

Watching the Hawks. (2017h). 'Informing vs Preaching in the News Media', *RT*, 19 January [Online]. Available at: https://youtu.be/ahdkQQUXSNg (Accessed: 16 November 2020).

Watching the Hawks. (2017i). 'The Plot to Scapegoat Russia', *RT*, 15 May [Online]. Available at: https://youtu.be/FlAnIQCNZrY (Accessed: 16 November 2020).

Watching the Hawks. (2017j). 'The New Old Cold War & The Reality of U.S. Foreign Policy', *RT*, 1 June [Online]. Available at: https://youtu.be/80iny0 yrZoM (Accessed: 16 November 2020).

Watching the Hawks. (2017k). 'Where's the Gate in Russiagate?', *RT*, 13 July [Online]. Available at: https://youtu.be/X90HX4a79F0 (Accessed: 16 November 2020).

Watching the Hawks. (2017l). 'Protecting the Future & Deep Facebook State', *RT*, 19 October [Online]. Available at: https://youtu.be/Xgd0NzvzrBQ (Accessed: 16 November 2020).

Watching the Hawks. (2017m). 'Russia, Wikileaks, and Snowden w/ Edward Jay Epstein', *RT*, 14 March [Online]. Available at: https://youtu.be/jSvmI3LQDYU (Accessed: 16 November 2020).

Watching the Hawks. (2017n). 'Press Freedom Flounders', *RT*, 29 November [Online]. Available at: https://youtu.be/EcgipyIyR1U (Accessed: 16 November 2020).

Watching the Hawks. (2017o). 'The Game of Hacks & Unmasking Guccifer / Unhacking the DNC Hack w/ Ray McGovern', *RT*, 3 August [Online]. Available at: https://www.rt.com/shows/watching-the-hawks/398568-hacker-drama-hbo-usa/ (Accessed: 17 November, 2020).

Watching the Hawks. (2018a). 'Ramadan Mubarak, Happy Birthday Russiagate (E723)', *RT*, 18 May [Online]. Available at: https://www.rt.com/shows/watching-the-hawks/427068-russiagate-probe-lee-stranahan/ (Accessed: 17 November 2020).

Watching the Hawks. (2018b). 'On the Receiving End of Russiagate with Randy Credico', *RT*, 12 January [Online]. Available at: https://youtu.be/s3mO-X9pDkg (Accessed: 16 November 2020).

5   Conspiracy and crisis

Narrative holes and the Skripal affair

Russia's current political leadership has become adept at employing the media as a tool of regime legitimation (Petrov et al., 2014; Tolz and Teper, 2018; Chatterje-Doody and Tolz, 2020. There is a temptation to view such instrumental uses of the media as part of a complex top-down strategy of political media management. Yet, Kremlin control over the media has developed in a chaotic fashion, and the global real-time media environment makes any effective top-down management of media narratives difficult. Nowhere is this clearer than during 'disruptive media events' (Katz and Liebes, 2007; Dayan, 2009; Figenschou and Thorbjørnsrud, 2016) – unwelcome and unanticipated occurrences which the political establishment cannot control. Often these events have a national security component and they tend to lead to a rapid circulation of contrasting opinions from multiple actors to global audiences through various digital media platforms (Hoskins and O'Loughlin, 2010; Tufekci, 2017). At these times, journalists at state-funded international broadcasters might be expected to doggedly follow their sponsor state's preferred narrative. In reality, though, they and their political masters have to react rapidly to evolving developments. Rapidly changing reports and reactions often ensue, based on minimal factual information and with no overall coherence. Such a situation makes it well-nigh impossible for any state to exert effective narrative control; it is also ripe for the development of conspiracy theories.

The March 2018 poisonings in the UK city of Salisbury provide the perfect example of this phenomenon. On 5 March, the local police force in Wiltshire declared a major incident, and London's Metropolitan Police announced shortly thereafter that a 'nerve agent' had been used against a male and female victim, later identified as the former Russian-British double agent Sergei Skripal and his daughter, Yulia. Just over a week later, British Prime Minister Theresa May announced in Parliament that it was 'highly likely that Russia was responsible' for 'attempted murder using a weapons-grade nerve agent... [in] an indiscriminate and reckless act against the United Kingdom' (CNN, 2018). The situation rapidly evolved into a full-scale diplomatic incident. Russia's Foreign Minister Sergei Lavrov likened the 'highly likely' attribution of blame to the reasoning of Lewis Carrol's Queen of Hearts in *Alice in Wonderland* (Ministry of Foreign Affairs, 2018). Nonetheless, before the month was out, the UK and allies had coordinated the largest ever mass expulsion of Russian diplomats – allegedly intelligence officers – in history (Dewan et al., 2018). Russia responded with expulsions of its own.

The Skripal saga continued throughout 2018, with each successive development in the case generating rafts of media coverage and speculation.[1] In early April, Russian state domestic television aired audio recordings of a telephone conversation between Yulia Skripal, still in hospital, and her cousin Viktoria, back in Russia, shortly before Yulia, and later Sergei, was quietly released from hospital. On 12 April, the Organization for the Prohibition of Chemical Weapons (OPCW) publicly released their summary report of findings following testing of the substance used, which 'confirm[ed] the findings of the United Kingdom relating to the identity of the toxic chemical that was used in Salisbury' (OPCW, 2018, article 10), with the name and structure of the chemical being included in the classified full report released to state members of the OPCW. All the while, there was significant public speculation in both the UK and Russia about the secrecy over the Skripals' release from hospital. Senior Russian government figures complained that they had been denied consular access to the pair and Yulia Skripal released a video statement via Reuters in late May. In it, she had visibly lost weight, and bore an apparent tracheotomy scar on her neck. She discussed how difficult the poisoning and recovery had been for her and her father, declined Russian consular assistance and asked for the Skripals' privacy to be respected (Faulconbridge, 2018). The following month, further poisonings were reported in neighbouring Amesbury. These ultimately led to the death of a local woman, Dawn Sturgess, who – as it later transpired – had sprayed herself with a perfume bottle containing a Novichok nerve agent (Morris and Rawlison, 2018).

In early September, British police charged two suspects with committing the poisonings, releasing their CCTV images and aliases: Ruslan Boshirov and Alexander Petrov. President Vladimir Putin stated unequivocally on 12 September that 'We know who they are, we found them', that the two men were civilians, and that he hoped that they would choose to tell their story (quoted in Luhn and Boyle, 2018). Just 24 hours later, the two men appeared in an exclusive interview with RT, which was both broadcast and released for online audiences on YouTube simultaneously in Russian and with English subtitles. Extracts were later broadcast on domestic channel Rossiia news, and with English dubbing on RT news. In the interview, RT's Editor-in-Chief, Margarita Simonyan, quizzed the suspects about their short trip to Salisbury, from which so many CCTV pictures had been released. The network's official explanation for the interview was that the men had voluntarily approached Simonyan via her callout on social media, and that RT was simply the broadcaster fortunate enough to bring this 'exclusive' to the public (Ruptly, 2018).

The men's story was that they were nutritional supplements' salesmen who had taken a sightseeing trip to Salisbury cathedral on the advice of friends, but whose plans had been derailed by inclement weather. Being caught up in the subsequent spy scandal was a nightmare that had ruined their lives. Online audiences were overwhelmingly disbelieving of their claims (Chatterje-Doody and Crilley, 2018; Tolz et al., 2020), and sure enough, in late September and early October, the open source investigative journalism outfit, *Bellingcat*, released the results of their collaborative investigations with the Russian investigative journalists of *The Insider* (Tolz, 2018). These revealed the true identities of 'Boshirov' and 'Petrov' as the decorated GRU (Russian military intelligence) agents Colonel Anatoly Chepiga and Dr Alexander Mishkin.

New developments in the case arose as part of an almost constant cycle, which served to sustain public interest. Yet, much of the crucial information was either sensitive or classified, and the UK and Russian governments made directly contradictory representations about the case and its aftermath. Together, RT and Sputnik promulgated a vast array of 'competing and often contradictory narratives' (Ramsay and Robertshaw, 2018, p. 6) about the poisoning and many conspiracy theories subsequently arose. They were often grounded in the official statements of either side, but did not necessarily hang coherently together.

In reporting developments in the Skripal case, RT often presented gaps in information (which were frequent given that it was classified) as evidence of an elite cover-up. As we have seen in previous chapters, the network's standard approach to such ideas is not usually by explicitly alleging that official accounts were fabricated, but by featuring guest commentators who raise sufficient questions as to imply that official accounts are problematic; RT's sister outlet, Sputnik, was often more blatant in its insinuations (Birge and Chatterje-Doody, 2021). In putting together its coverage, RT drew upon social media content produced by members of the public and wove together grassroots vox populi commentary; perspectives from British institutional margins; speculation from online analytical sources; social media comments and the bombastic contributions of noted conspiracy theorists. The sheer volume of conspiratorial readings featured within RT's coverage of the Skripal affair makes it impractical to comprehensively trace them all: there are many overlaps in the conspiracy logics that they display, yet there is rarely a logical coherence between them. Nonetheless, the remainder of the chapter outlines in more detail three broad strands of conspiracy logic that recurred in RT's coverage: the UK was complicit in the case for domestic political reasons; the key actors in the case are not what they seem and there has been an internationally co-ordinated cover-up.

UK complicity

At various points, RT's coverage suggested that the UK was directly involved in the poisonings. In the early stages of breaking the poisoning story, RT relied extensively for its expert commentary on 'former intelligence officers and diplomats turned whistle-blower' (Birge and Chatterje-Doody, 2021) whose own prior experiences afforded them a particularly negative vision of UK security institutions. Elements of the British government explanation were consistently questioned, implying official accounts could not be trusted (RT, 2018c, 2018d).

Often, the impetus for these suggestions came directly from the Russian political establishment. For instance, on 10 April, following Yulia's discharge from hospital, the Russian Embassy in the UK tweeted to congratulate her on her recovery. It also requested 'urgent proof that what is being done to her is being done on her own free will', and accused the UK of 'destroying important and valuable evidence' by destroying the Skripals' pets and the bench on which they had initially been taken ill (Grierson, 2018). Political bloggers subsequently engaged in considerable conspiracy theorising about the brief statement released at her discharge. One of the commentators making this suggestion was Craig Murray, a former UK Ambassador and frequent RT guest (Murray, 2018). Other political bloggers speculated on the reasons for the Skripals' public silence (Moon of Alabama, 2018a). This kind of conspiratorial speculation was amplified following the release of Yulia Skripal's 23 May video statement via Reuters, with some labelling it a 'hostage video' (Moon of Alabama, 2018b). Craig

Murray explicitly reiterated his allegation that she was held under duress in another blog post that formed the central source for an RT web report the following day (RT, 2018p).

At other times, RT simply reported the explicitly conspiratorial allegations made by senior politicians. These included comments from Foreign Minister, Sergei Lavrov, that the substance used in the attack was not Novichok, but BZ – more commonly used by the US and UK (RT, 2018j) and from the Russian Foreign Ministry spokesperson, Maria Zakharova, that the poisonings were a 'false-flag incident... beneficial for, or perhaps organized by, the British intelligence services in order to mar Russia and its political leadership' (RT, 2018m).[2] RT took a similar line in reporting the comments of Russia's permanent representative to the OPCW, when he alleged that the UK has systematically lied about various aspects of the case (RT, 2018n).

The centrality of external sources for these conspiracy theories is crucial to understand how RT reported these case developments, especially given that the network was at this point being extensively investigated by the British regulator, Ofcom, as had been announced on 18 April (Ofcom, 2018a). Much of RT's reporting, therefore, was structured around accurate reports of the fears and allegations that had been expressed elsewhere, rather than as allegations made from the editorial voice (RT, 2018p). However, as part of this pattern, entire articles were often constructed around extensive quotes from singular sources (RT, 2018r). In other cases, reporting was bulked out with social media users' conspiratorial readings of the situation, giving the impression that there was public consensus around their reported feelings that 'This is a hostage video' or simply that 'Something doesn't add up!' (RT, 2018q).

Some of RT's extended broadcast programmes took a similar approach to discussing the case. Guests on RT UK's political discussion show, 'Going Underground' raised questions about official reports through a debate in which the British presenter played a 'devil's advocate' position of ostensibly supporting the British position. At other times, however, conspiracy theories were liberally and extensively explored. One of the most notable examples of this was in an episode of *CrossTalk* provocatively entitled 'Publicity Murder?' (RT, 2018e). In its usual fashion, the show brought together a series of guests with almost identical perspectives on the case, together with a clearly biased presenter, who delivered many impassioned monologues straight to camera. The programme mooted various theories, including the idea that Novichok could be made relatively widely and easily (including, by implication, in the UK); that Skripal had no remaining strategic value to Russia, which therefore had no motive and that the timing of the poisoning – before Russia's Presidential elections and hosting of the FIFA World Cup – cast suspicion on those negatively disposed to the country.

Despite these cyclical insinuations of UK complicity in the case, the network nonetheless published a striking 'double bluff' courtesy of Putin himself, who stated his own belief that it was unlikely that the British government committed the crime (RT, 2019d). On the one hand, this story can be seen as part of a performance to dispel accusations of conspiracy theorising; on the other hand, it is worth noting that news consumers are more likely to believe false claims the more often they are exposed to them, even if the repetition comes as part of a retraction (Swire et al., 2017; Pennycook et al 2018a). A denial such as this then could easily strengthen the narrative of UK complicity, which RT was periodically returning to fully two years after the case (RT, 2019b; Rite, 2020).

The key actors are not what they seem

Over the course of RT's Skripal coverage, the credibility and plausibility of political actors and their accounts was undermined within a recurring idea that actors and organisations assumed to be independent or authoritative commentators on the case were actually motivated by their own interlinked interests. RT dismissed the many leaks from unverifiable anonymous 'intelligence sources' about the case as evidence of widespread Russophobia and poor journalistic standards in the Western mainstream media (Rite, 2019). Similarly conspiratorial allegations were reported by RT about the off-duty nurse who treated the Skripals at the scene, and who turned out to be the chief nursing officer in the British Army – a fact described by RT as 'unlikely' (RT, 2018f).

In several cases, RT used conspiracy theories to discredit the key institutions tasked with establishing the facts around the case. For instance, early on, it reported claims from the Russian Foreign Ministry that the UK government had pressured the Metropolitan police during the investigation (RT, 2018x). When the Metropolitan police made clear that it would be extremely difficult to establish a chain of evidence sufficient to prove that the order for the attack had come from the top of the Russian political establishment, RT framed this as a general admission of a lack of evidence in the case (RT, 2019f).

The UK government's testing facility at Porton Down – described as 'the chief British chemical and bioweapons laboratory' (RT, 2019b) – and the OPCW, whose investigation processes had supported Porton

Down's findings, were both discredited in RT's reporting. RT constructed a whole web report around claims by Russia's Ambassador to the UK that the OPCW's verification of Porton Down's findings was controlled by Britain, conducted suspiciously quickly, was not transparent and breached the parameters of the Chemical Weapons Convention (CWC) (RT, 2018o). RT further reported suggestions by both Russia's Embassy to the UK, and a former FSB Chief, that a leak from Porton Down might be responsible for the Salisbury and Amesbury poisonings (RT, 2018v, 2018w). By suggesting a conspiracy between the official institutions involved in investigating the case, RT's reporting also opened up space to question the key facts that had been established. A series of web reports in mid-April quoted senior Russian politicians' suggestions that the substance used in the attack was not Novickok, but BZ – a substance whose use was more associated with the US and UK than with Russia (RT, 2018j, 2018k, 2018l). The following year, an RT op-ed speculated whether the substance used had been fentanyl (Clark, 2019).

The same conspiracy lenses were applied when, Russia's *The Insider* and their UK-based collaborators, *Bellingcat* used open sources, leaked information and old-fashioned investigative journalism, to identify 'Petrov' and 'Boshirov' as military intelligence operatives, later revealing their names as Colonel Chepiga and Dr Mishkin (Tolz, 2018). Despite the saturation coverage that RT had given to the suspects' initial interview, its coverage of *The Insider/Bellingcat* reveal was fairly minimal, and the role of independent investigative journalists at *The Insider* was ignored: they would have been difficult to discredit given the privilege that RT generally affords to independent and freelance investigative journalists over establishment mainstream media representatives. RT's scant coverage of this development noted that the 'authenticity and veracity of the documents' used by *Bellingcat* 'could not be immediately verified' (RT, 2018z), with subsequent articles suggesting that funding from actors including the 'US government-funded' National Endowment for Democracy; 'British intelligence agencies' and the 'pro-NATO Atlantic Council think tank' dictated *Bellingcat*'s investigative priorities and conclusions (RT, 2018za). There have been subsequent suggestions that *Bellingcat* contributors are sullied by association with the UK government-backed Integrity Initiative, described by RT as 'a clandestine propaganda outlet' (RT, 2019a). In its follow-up reporting of the Skripal case, RT (2020a) continued to cast doubt on *Bellingcat*'s professionalism and – by implication – the validity of its findings about the suspects, referring to *Bellingcat* as a 'controversial internet sleuth shop'.

Russia as the West's scapegoat

One of the key recurring themes on RT when covering any stories that involve international criticisms of Russia is that they are motivated by Russophobic prejudice. In the very early days after the Skripal poisoning story, RT reported the connection in precisely this way, with early headlines declaring 'Blame precedes evidence' (RT, 2018a; see also RT 2018b). Similar insinuations were repeated in a variety of ways as the story progressed. These included direct allegations that political figures were invested in the poisoning furore as a way to sabotage Russia's hosting of the 2018 World Cup (RT, 2018e, 2018f). There were also various allusions to the similarities between the Skripal case and fictional spy stories (Birge and Chatterje-Doody, 2021). Citing both classic examples and those from more recent television history, the most favourable implication of these allusions was that of a lack of imagination on the part of key Western powers; the least favourable was that these similarities suggested suspicious activity (see RT News, 2018). With Russophobia being one of RT's recurring editorial lines, it is unsurprising that this theme continued to recur throughout the case.

The coordinated international expulsions of alleged Russian intelligence operatives that followed the poisonings were interpreted as part of a globally coordinated attempt to smear Russia, with one commentator suggesting they revealed the hand of the 'deep state' in helping a corrupt elite to hold on power (RT, 2018h). Where RT's own presenter, George Galloway (RT, 2018g) referred to the expulsions acts of 'vassal states' (Europe) or acts of war (US), external commentators painted the case as providing a 'pretext' for a hypocritical group of Western powers to pursue a 'new Cold War... more dangerous than the old Cold War' (RT, 2018i). RT itself became a subject of these discussions of rampant Russophobia, after British politicians suggested stricter media regulation of the channel, and an appearance boycott. The network insinuated that this could be a step towards consideration of a ban (RT, 2018zb, 2018zc).

Some of RT's contributors relied on far more extreme conspiracy theories, based on assumptions of premeditation and deceit. By the end of May 2018, a regular contributor to both RT and Sputnik, Neil Clark was raising questions about whether the poisoning had even taken place. His speculation was prompted by the revelation that a Russian journalist thought murdered in Ukraine by Kremlin operatives was alive and well. Making a surprise appearance at a press conference called to discuss his murder, Arkadii Babchenko announced that he had collaborated with Ukrainian security services to stage his death in order to foil a genuine plot on his life. In an op-ed for Sputnik, Clark used the exposure of this genuine conspiracy as evidence that allegations against Russia in the Skripal case were driven by conspirators: 'the faking of Babchenko's death should make us wonder what else has been fabricated in pursuance of the neocons' anti-Russian geopolitical agenda' (Clark, 2018). RT's own coverage used the Babchenko case to highlight unethical methods in targeted action against Russia, as well as to cast doubt on the trustworthiness of intelligence services and journalists alike (RT, 2018s, 2018t, 2018u).

Conclusion

In reporting this most intriguing of cases, RT's coverage insinuated conspiracies of many types, centred around governments, journalists, professional scientists and international organisations. Many of these conspiracy theories were inconsistent with one another, and changed vastly over time. Yet, their key function appeared not so much to establish a coherent alternative narrative for how and why the Salisbury poisonings took place, nor who was responsible. Rather, these conspiracy theories worked together to chip away at the credibility of the official accounts that had been released to the public about the poisonings.

However, many of the conspiracy theories alluded to on RT did not arise in the first place on the network. Rather, due to the security implications of disruptive media events such as the poisoning of the Skripals, high public interest is stymied by low public information. Speculation becomes rife, and RT is particularly adept at trading in this. RT showed a conscious effort to clearly attribute controversial claims to sources outside of the network itself, but gave them disproportionate coverage in expanded stories generated out of these often small and specific interventions.

With this in mind, it is worth noting that such conspiracy theories can come both from the political blogosphere, and via direct quotation of senior Russian politicians. Key Ministry and Embassy officials and social media accounts habitually articulated conspiracy theories in respect of the Skripal case, which RT subsequently reported faithfully as newsworthy comments. Even though appropriate journalistic standards of accuracy may be applied in the strictest sense, such practices nonetheless work to spread conspiracy theories. What is more, in some cases, these perspectives and allegations were presented as balancing the official UK line. As the ruling of the UK media regulator, Ofcom's (2018b) investigation into RT emphasised, however – reiterating conclusions from its 2016 investigation of *CrossTalk* – such techniques may not necessarily provide sufficient balance on a case of such high controversy. Ofcom therefore ruled against RT in respect of seven programmes, and imposed a substantial fine (Hutchings et al, 2018). However, RT has responded by pursuing a judicial review on the grounds that the relevant guidelines were not sufficiently clear or reliable.

Given that Ofcom's stipulated sanctions fell short of a licence revocation, RT's pursuit of this review demonstrates that the maintenance of the broadcast licence is not its only concern in the UK. It also seeks to maintain some level of reputation whilst questioning Ofcom's own impartiality and reliability – thus shielding RT from some of its criticisms. Indeed, this issue recurred in the aftermath of the 2020 release of the Russia report by the UK's Intelligence and Security Select Committee, with RT reporting scathingly on MPs' calls for Ofcom to review RT's broadcast licence as an example of improper political interference in the media (RT, 2020b). In this way, conspiracy theories about Russophobia and corruption amongst interlinked political and media elites recurs throughout RT's reporting, even as the news cycle moves on.

Notes

1 For a comprehensive analysis of Russian journalists' responses to the Skripal poisoning domestically and internationally, see Tolz et al. (2020); and for analysis of how Russian international broadcasters presented it for international audiences, see Birge and Chatterje-Doody (2021).
2 This accusation was repeated the following year, e.g. https://www.rt.com/news/452946-skripal-anniversary-truth-novichok/ Salisbury poisoning: One year on, still no evidence of Novichok nerve agent use disclosed to public, 4 March 2019.

References

Birge, L. and Chatterje-Doody, P.N. (2021). 'Russian Public Diplomacy: Questioning Certainties in Uncertain Times', in P. Surowiec and I. Manor (eds.) *Public Diplomacy and the Politics of Uncertainty*. London: Palgrave, pp. 171–195.

Chatterje-Doody, P.N. and Crilley, R. (2018). 'How Badly Did Russia's Interview with the Skripal Suspects Backfire?', *The Washington Post Monkey Cage*, September 15 [Online]. Available at: https://www.washingtonpost.com/gdpr-consent/?destination=%2fnews%2fmonkey-cage%2fwp%2f2018%2f09%2f15%2fhow-badly-did-russias-interview-with-the-skripal-poisoning-suspects-backfire%2f%3f (Accessed: 16 November 2020).

Chatterje-Doody, P.N. and Tolz, V. (2020). 'Regime Legitimation, Not Nation-Building: Media Commemoration of the 1917 Revolutions in Russia's Neo-authoritarian State', *European Journal of Cultural Studies*, 23(3), pp. 335–353.

Clark, N. (2018). 'How Much Else Has Been Faked', *Sputnik*, 1 June [Online]. Available at: https://sputniknews.com/columnists/201806011065009180-arkady-babchenko-murder-faked/ (Accessed: 17 November 2020).

Clark, N. (2019). 'Let's Not Make a Drama about Skripal Case before Important Questions Are Answered Op-ed', *RT*, May 22 [Online]. Available at: https://www.rt.com/op-ed/460005-skripal-novichok-questions-poisoning/ (Accessed: 17 November 2020).

Dayan, D. (2009). 'Beyond Media Events: Disenchantment, Derailment, Disruption', in N. Couldry, A. Hepp, and F. Krotz (eds.) *Media Events in a Global Age*. London: Routledge, pp. 391–402.

Dewan, A., Veselinovic, M., and Jordan, C. (2018). 'These Are All the Countries That Are Expelling Russian Diplomats', *CNN*, 28 March [Online]. Available at: https://edition.cnn.com/2018/03/26/europe/full-list-of-russian-diplomats-expelled-over-s-intl/index.html (Accessed: 04 March 2020).

Faulconbridge, G. (2018). 'Exclusive: Yulia Skripal - Attempted Assassination Turned My World Upside Down', *Reuters*, 23 May [Online]. Available at: https://uk.reuters.com/article/uk-britain-russia-skripal-yulia-exclusiv/exclusive-yulia-skripal-attempted-assassination-turned-my-world-upside-down-idUKKCN1IO2L5 (Accessed: on 16 November 2020).

Figenschou, U.T. and Thorbjørnsrud, K. (2016). 'Disruptive Media Events', *Journalism Practice*, 11(8), pp. 942–959.

Grierson, J. (2018). 'Yulia Skripal Discharged from Hospital after Salisbury Attack', *The Guardian*, 10 April [Online]. Available at: https://www.theguardian.com/uk-news/2018/apr/10/yulia-skripal-discharged-from-hospital-salisbury-attack-nerve-agent (Accessed 05 March 2020).

Hoskins, A. and O'Loughlin, B. (2010). *War and Media: The Emergence of Diffused War*. Cambridge: Polity Press.

Hutchings, S., Crilley, R., and Chatterje-Doody, P.N. (2018). 'Ofcom's Latest Ruling on RT Is More Significant than You Might Think', *The Huffington Post*, 21 December [Online]. Available at: https://www.huffingtonpost.co.uk/entry/ofcom-rt-bbc-latest_uk_5c1ce1b8e4b08aaf7a87c17c (Accessed: 17 November 2020).

Katz, E. and Liebes, T. (2007). '"No More Peace!': How Disaster, Terror and War Have Upstaged Media Events', *International Journal of Communication*, 1(1), pp. 157–166.

Luhn, A. and Boyle, D. (2018). 'Vladimir Putin Says Salisbury Poison Suspects Are Russian 'Civilians' and Hopes They Will 'Tell Their Story'', *The Telegraph*, 12 September [Online]. Available at: https://www.telegraph.co.uk/news/2018/09/12/vladimir-putin-says-russia-has-identified-salisbury-poisonsuspects/ (Accessed: 04 March 2020).

Moon of Alabama. (2018a). 'The Silence of the Skripals - Government Blocks Press Reports - Media Change the Record', *Moon of Alabama*, 28 April [Online]. Available at: https://www.moonofalabama.org/2018/04/the-silence-of-the-skripals-government-blocks-press-reports-media-change-the-record.html (Accessed: 17 November 2020).

Moon of Alabama. (2018b). 'British Hostage Video of Yulia Skripal Released', *Moon of Alabama*, 24 May [Online]. Available at: https://www.moonof alabama.org/2018/05/hostage-video-of-yulia-skripal-released.html (Accessed: 17 November 2020).

Morris, S. and Rawlison, K. (2018). 'Novichok Victim Found Substance Disguised as Perfume in Sealed Box', *The Guardian*, 24 July [Online]. Available at: https://www.theguardian.com/uk-news/2018/jul/24/novichok-victim-ill-within-15-minutes-says-partner-charlie-rowley (Accessed: 17 November 2020).

Ministry of Foreign Affairs. (2018). Foreign Minister Sergey Lavrov's Interview with BBC HardTalk. Available at: https://www.mid.ru/en/press_service/minister_speeches/-/asset_publisher/7OvQR5KJWVmR/content/id/3172318 (Accessed: 17 November 2020).

Murray, C. (2018). 'Yulia Skripal Is Plainly under Duress', *Craig Murray*, 11 April. Available at: https://www.craigmurray.org.uk/archives/2018/04/yulia-skripal-is-plainly-under-duress/. (Accessed: 05 March 2020).

Ofcom. (2018a). Update on RT News Channel. Available at: https://www.ofcom.org.uk/about-ofcom/latest/features-and-news/rt-update (Accessed: 05 March 2020).

Ofcom. (2018b). Ofcom Broadcast and On Demand Bulletin, Issue 369, 20 December [Online]. Available at: https://www.ofcom.org.uk/__data/assets/pdf_file/0020/131159/Issue-369-Broadcast-and-On-Demand-Bulletin.pdf (Accessed: 18 November 2020).

OPCW. (2018). Summary of the Report on Activities Carried out in Support of a Request for Technical Assistance by the United Kingdom of Great Britain and Northern Ireland (Technical Assistance Visit TAV/02/18) Note no. S/1612/2018. Available at: https://www.opcw.org/sites/default/files/documents/S_series/2018/en/s-1612-2018_e_.pdf (Accessed: 04 March 2020).

Pennycook, G., Cannon, T., and Rand, D.G. (2018a). 'Prior Exposure Increases Perceived Accuracy of Fake News', *Journal of Experimental Psychology: General*, 147(12), pp. 1865–1880.

Petrov, N., Lipman, M., and Hale, H.E. (2014). 'Three Dilemmas of Hybrid Regime Governance: Russia from Putin to Putin', *Post-Soviet Affairs*, 30(1), pp. 1–26.

Ramsay, G. and Robertshaw, S. (2018). Weaponising News: RT, Sputnik and Targeted Disinformation. King's College London: The Policy Institute. Available at: https://www.kcl.ac.uk/policy-institute/assets/weaponising-news.pdf.

Rite, S. (2019). "Anonymous Intelligence Sources' Thrive in post-Skripal Limelight', *RT*, 4 March [Online]. Available at: https://www.rt.com/

uk/452987-anonymous-intelligence-sources-skripal/ (Accessed: 17 November 2020).

Rite, Simon (2020) 'Salisbury poisoning unleashed Russian bogeyman ... but where are the Skripals 2 years on?' RT 4 March 2020, Available at: https://www. rt.com/op-ed/482319-skripals-britain-russia-poisoning-spy/ (Accessed: 16 April 2021).

RT. (2018a). 'Blame Precedes Evidence as Western Media Speculates Freely over Ill Russian Spy (VIDEO)', *RT*, 6 March [Online]. Available at: https:// www.rt.com/uk/420607-skripal-russophobia-spy-kremlin/ (Accessed: 17 November 2020).

RT. (2018b). 'Boris Johnson Threatens Sanctions before Any Evidence of Russian Links to Ex-spy's Illness', *RT*, 6 March [Online]. Available at: https:// www.rt.com/uk/420602-uk-russian-double-agent/ (Accessed: 17 November 2020).

RT. (2018c). 'Russia Has 'No Motive' to Attempt Murder of Ex-spy, George Galloway Tells RT', *RT*, 6 March [Online]. Available at: https://www.rt.com/ uk/420639-russia-sergei-skripal-conspiracy/ (Accessed: 17 November 2020).

RT. (2018d). 'Moscow Is Open to Working with UK over Incident with Russian Ex-double Agent – Kremlin', *RT*, 6 March [Online]. Retrieved from https://www.rt.com/news/420618-kremlin-uk-former-spy/ (Accessed: 17 November 2020).

RT. (2018e). 'Publicity Murder?', *RT*, 14 March [Online]. Available at: https:// www.rt.com/shows/crosstalk/421220-uk-blame-russia-poison/ (Accessed: 17 November 2020).

RT. (2018f). 'Putin's World Cup Is like Hitler's 1936 Olympics – Boris Johnson (VIDEO)', *RT*, 21 March [Online]. Available at: https://www.rt.com/ uk/421930-boris-johnson-skripal-election/ (Accessed: 17 November 2020).

RT. (2018g). 'US Expulsion of Russian Diplomats Is 'Declaration of War' – George Galloway to RT', *RT*, 26 March [Online]. Available at: https://www. rt.com/news/422385-expulsion-russian-diplomats-galloway/ (Accessed: 17 November 2020).

RT. (2018h). 'Wave of Russian Diplomat Expulsions Is Coordinated Political Warfare against Moscow', *RT*, 27 March [Online]. Available at: https:// www.rt.com/news/422469-diplomat-expulsions-political-warfare/ (Accessed: 17 November 2020).

RT. (2018i). ''No Guarantee We Will Survive This New Cold War' – Peter Kuznick', *RT*, 28 March [Online]. Available at: https://www.rt.com/ news/422588-us-uk-diplomat-expulsion/ (Accessed: 17 November 2020).

RT. (2018j). 'Lavrov: Swiss Lab Says 'BZ Toxin' Used in Salisbury, not Produced in Russia, Was in US & UK Service', *RT*, 14 April [Online]. Available at: https://www.rt.com/news/424149-skripal-poisoning-bz-lavrov/ (Accessed: 17 November 2020).

RT. (2018k). 'OPCW-accredited Swiss Lab Can 'Neither Confirm nor Deny' BZ Toxin Was Used in Skripal Poisoning', *RT*, 16 April [Online]. Available at: https://www.rt.com/news/424278-opcw-spiez-lab-comment/ (Accessed: 17 November 2020).

RT. (2018l). 'London Should Face Uncomfortable Questions from G7 over Skripal Poisoning – Russian Senator', *RT*, 17 April [Online]. Available at: https://www.rt.com/russia/424354-london-questions-skripal-pushkov/ (Accessed: 17 November 2020).

RT. (2018m). 'Skripals Poisoning 'Highly Likely' Staged By British Intelligence – Russian Foreign Ministry', *RT*, 19 April [Online]. Available at: https://www.rt.com/news/424612-skripal-poisoning-british-spies-moscow/ (Accessed: 17 November 2020).

RT. (2018n). 'Russia's OPCW Envoy Exposes 'Eight UK Lies' in Skripal Case', *RT*, 19 April [Online]. Available at: https://www.rt.com/news/424537-russia-opcw-uk-skripal-lies/ (Accessed: 17 November 2020).

RT. (2018o). 'OPCW Work on Skripal Poisoning Lacks Transparency – Russian Envoy to UK', *RT*, 20 April [Online]. Available at: https://www.rt.com/uk/424702-skripal-opcw-uk-transparency/ (Accessed: 17 November 2020).

RT. (2018p). 'Skripals May Be Kept in UK against Their Will – Russian Foreign Minister', *RT*, 23 May [Online]. Available at: https://www.rt.com/news/427499-skripal-held-uk-against-will (Accessed: 17 November 2020).

RT. (2018q). 'Russian Diplomats Must Be Allowed Access to Yulia Skripal to Know She's Not Held Forcibly – Embassy', *RT*, 23 May [Online]. Available at: https://www.rt.com/news/427580-embassy-yulia-skripal-access/ (Accessed: 17 November 2020).

RT. (2018r). ''Duress Cannot Be Ruled Out': ex-UK Ambassador Craig Murray Unconvinced By Yulia Skripal Interview', *RT*, 24 May [Online]. Available at: https://www.rt.com/uk/427648-skripal-craig-murray-interview/ (Accessed: 17 November 2020).

RT. (2018s). ''Assassinated' Journalist Babchenko Alive, Kiev Accuses Russian Intelligence of Murder Plot', *RT*, 30 May [Online]. Available at: https://www.rt.com/news/428240-babchenko-alive-special-operation/ (Accessed: 17 November 2020).

RT. (2018t). 'Babchenko's Fake Murder in Ukraine Part of 'Lamentable Campaign Targeting Russia'', *RT*, 31 May [Online]. Available at: https://www.rt.com/news/428368-ukraine-babchenko-fake-murder/ (Accessed: 17 November 2020).

RT. (2018u). 'Kiev's Fake Babchenko Murder Erodes Media & Information Credibility – Intl Journalist Federation', *RT*, 31 May [Online]. Available at: https://www.rt.com/news/428393-babchenko-fake-murder-inappropriate/ (Accessed: 17 November 2020).

RT. (2018v). ''UK Has Problems with Securing Poisonous Agents' – Former FSB Chief', *RT*, 5 July, [Online]. Available at: https://www.rt.com/news/431787-uk-russia-poisoning-amesbury/ (Accessed: 17 November 2020).

RT. (2018w). 'Leak at Porton down Lab May be Behind UK Nerve-Agent Poisonings – Russian Embassy', *RT*, 14 July [Online]. Available at: https://

www.rt.com/uk/433109-porton-down-leak-novichok/ (Accessed: 17 November 2020).

RT. (2018x). 'UK Officials Harass Own Police in 'Novichok' Probes – Russia's Foreign Ministry', *RT*, 3 August [Online]. Available at: https://www.rt.com/news/435069-russia-foreign-ministry-police/ (Accessed: 17 November 2020).

RT. (2018z). 'Bellingcat Claims It 'Conclusively' Identified Skripal Poisoning Suspect as Decorated Commando', *RT*, 26 September [Online]. Available at: https://www.rt.com/uk/439556-bellingcat-identification-salisbury-suspect/ (Accessed: 17 November 2020).

RT. (2018za). 'Despite Mainstream Glory, Questions Raised about Bellingcat Authenticity and Skripal Poisoning Case', *RT*, 10 October [Online]. Available at: https://www.rt.com/uk/440899-bellingcat-authenticity-questions-media/ (Accessed: 17 November 2020).

RT. (2018zb). 'War on RT: Staunch anti-Russian MP Wants Special Powers for Ofcom (VIDEO)', *RT*, 28 June [Online]. Available at: https://www.rt.com/uk/431169-bob-seely-ofcom-tory/ (Accessed: 18 November 2020).

RT. (2018zc). 'Amesbury Poisoning Incident Fuels another Wave of anti-Russian Hysteria', *RT*, 5 July [Online]. Available at: http://www.rt.com/uk/431847-uk-rt-propaganda-free-speech/ (Accessed: 18 November 2020).

RT (2018). RT News - March 06, 2018 Available at: https://www.rt.com/shows/news/420626-rtnews-march-06-17msk/ (Accessed: 16 April 2021)

RT. (2019a). 'Bellingcat Activist Fails to Ban Blogger Who Exposed His Ties to UK Propaganda Outfit on Twitter', *RT*, 14 January [Online]. Available at: https://www.rt.com/news/448743-bellingcat-blogger-integraty-initiative-twitter/ (Accessed: 17 November 2020)

RT. (2019b). 'Salisbury Poisoning: One Year On, Still No Evidence of Novichok Nerve Agent Use Disclosed to Public', *RT*, 4 March [Online]. Available at: https://www.rt.com/news/452946-skripal-anniversary-truth-novichok/ (Accessed: 17 November 2020).

RT. (2019f). 'You Have to Prove Putin Was Involved': Met Police Push Back against UK Blame Game in Skripal Saga', *RT*, 8 August [Online]. Available at: https://www.rt.com/news/466089-skripals-uk-police-evidence/ (Accessed: 17 November 2020).

RT. (2020a). 'Free Press? Labour Letter Demands RT UK's License Gets REVOKED in Light of 'Damning' Russia Report That Gave NO Examples or Proof', RT, 23 July [Online]. Available at: https://www.rt.com/uk/495676-labour-stevens-letter-ofcom-rt/ (Accessed: 17 November 2020).

RT. (2020b). 'Probe into 'Novichok' Death of Dawn Sturgess Can Blame Russia, UK Judges Say, But 'No Trial Will Realistically Happen'', *RT*, 24 July [Online]. Available at: https://www.rt.com/uk/495793-sturgess-novichok-court-skripals/ (Accessed: 17 November 2020).

Ruptly. (2018). 'REFEED: RT Editor-in-chief Interviews Two Men UK Named as Suspects in Skripal Case', *RT*, 18 September [YouTube]. Available at: https://www.youtube.com/watch?v=38uqN5ypRWE&t=8s (Accessed: 17 November 2020).

Swire, B., Ecker, U.K.H. and Lewandowsky, S. (2017). 'The Role of Familiarity in Correcting Inaccurate Information', *Journal of Experimental Psychological Learning and Memory Cognition*, 43(12), pp. 1948–1961.

Tolz, V. (2018). 'Colonel Chepiga: Who Really Identified the Skripal Poisoner and Why It Matters', *The Conversation*, 3 October [Online]. Available at: https://theconversation.com/colonel-chepiga-who-really-identified-the-skripal-poisoner-and-why-it-matters-104275 (Accessed: 17 November 2020).

Tolz, V., Hutchings, S., Chatterje-Doody, P.N., and Crilley, R. (2020). 'Mediatization and Journalistic Agency: Russian Television Coverage of the Skripal Poisonings', *Journalism*. doi:10.1177/1464884920941967.

Tolz, V. and Teper, Y. (2018). 'Broadcasting Agitainment: A New Media Strategy of Putin's Third Presidency', *Post-Soviet Affairs*, 34(4), pp. 213–227.

Tufekci, Z. (2017). *Twitter and Tear Gas: The Power and Fragility of Networked Protest*. New Haven, CT: Yale University Press.

6 RT in the post-pandemic world

The year 2020 was a difficult year for the planet. The COVID-19 pandemic, the unfolding economic crisis, race riots in the US as well as the Presidential elections in November – all are issues that perfectly fit RT's list of preferred themes: global economic control by the super-rich; the corrupt political system of the US and the mainstream's media failure to report fairly on important news. It is at times like those of a pandemic or terrorist attack like 9/11, according to RT's hosts, that no one is watching what politicians are doing, enabling them to push forward all sorts of antidemocratic and anti-constitutional laws that increase the establishment's power (Watching the Hawks, 2020a). Yet, it is precisely these two main global events of 2020 that demonstrate the evolution that RT has undergone in the 15 years since its establishment.

Case 1: COVID-19 pandemic

For the sake of comparability with earlier chapters, we analysed the relevant broadcasts of the shows *Watching the Hawks*, *CrossTalk* and *The World According to Jesse* as well as news broadcasts and op-eds in the period from February to December 2020. COVID-19 was a central topic on all shows through late February–early May. The coverage of the stories directly related to the COVID-19 pandemic was largely in line with factual information from other US and European broadcasters. In their broadcasts RT's hosts focussed on the issues of social inequality, poor handling of the health crisis by authorities, Big Pharma lobbyism and the global establishment's ambitions to gain more power. The usual elite bashing by RT's hosts was mixed with stories critical of the various conspiracy theorists who saw the 'stay at home' rule as the federal government's conspiracy to lock down the population. *Watching the Hawks* hosts emphasised that Americans protesting against lockdown rules were not smart. The 'stay at home policy is not about liberty, it is about taking care of people' (Watching the Hawks, 2020b). This trend of coverage shows RT actively trying to maintain a reputation as a serious international media outlet, whilst still carefully leaving room for unrestrained conspiratorial rhetoric.

The Russian roots of the channel were very hard to identify in the post-pandemic coverage. As Tolz and Hutchings noted in their analysis, the Russian factor is crucial in finding conspiracy theories and misinformation in RT's broadcasts and becomes evident in times of international crises: 'During periods when Russian actions are not under the international spotlight, RT's coverage is more factually accurate and biases are less strongly pronounced than when it covers issues specifically related to Russia's policies' (Tolz and Hutchings, 2020). This is clearly seen in the first three months of the pandemic when COVID-19 was a top story across all media. Yet, when conspiracy theories regarding Russia's anti-COVID policies popped up accusing the Russian government of hiding the real counts of sick and dead people, RT reacted immediately. 'Russia is not hiding any cases of COVID, despite conspiracy theories spread in the western press', said the correspondent, referencing the interview of the WHO Russia representative. The message of the report was that the Russian government was handling the crisis perfectly well, whilst foreign governments that failed to protect their own citizens tried to destroy Russia's image (RT, 2020a). A similar tone was taken when the Western media questioned the efficiency of the Russian Sputnik vaccine that was the first registered COVID vaccine in the world (BBC News, 2020). RT's commentators first questioned Big Pharma's actions and accused these companies of bribing medics (Frawley, 2020), then accused Big Pharma of paying the media for unashamedly bashing Russia's pioneering and effective drug (Ferrada de Noli, 2020).

However, the central element of RT's agenda – the blame game against 'mainstream media' – put it in a difficult position. Whilst most of the major media in the US were very cautious of COVID 19 from the start of the year and emphasised how dangerous the disease could be for humans, RT's take on this put some hosts into a problematic situation. On 29 February at the start of the outbreak, RT's hosts pushed the idea that mainstream media were overreacting. 'Media love stories like that' (The World According to Jesse, 2020a). Jimmy Dore – a co-host of Jesse Ventura's show – advocated not reacting, and not buying what the media is selling. Lavelle in *CrossTalk* opined that the coronavirus was used by Western governments and media as a weapon of global information war against China and Russia (CrossTalk, 2020a). Around the same time, Lavelle's guests accused Western corporate elites of running a coup against public safety. One of his guests accused the media in the UK and the US of being the main beneficiaries of the coronavirus: they should have reported the whole danger of the virus, but waited until the pandemic reached the global size to enjoy increased audience interest (CrossTalk, 2020b).

On 7 March, as the pandemic was developing, Jesse Ventura's show hosts made a small correction following the WHO that the number of cases globally was rising. Hosts made the point that information was coming from China, which controls its media. They diverted the conversation to the regular suspects: governments who cannot be trusted when it comes to delivering information; they will put us – concerned citizens – in a situation where we can be fooled (The World According to Jesse, 2020b). On 21 March Jesse Ventura's co-host Brigida Santos announced that the number of people in the studio had been massively decreased to follow government recommendations and the tone of the programmes became more careful (The World According to Jesse, 2020c).

One of the central topics of RT's coverage of the COVID 19 pandemic is how big business and the federal government have profited from it. 'Profits over people' was a tag line for many shows (Watching the Hawks, 2020c). Tyrel Ventura's opening speeches in 'Watching the Hawks' were often focussed on how corrupt and manipulative the US establishment revealed itself to be during the pandemic. Stories discussed in RT's shows at the time constantly focussed on social polarisation and pushed the populist criticism of the pandemic social divide (The World According to Jesse, 2020d). The US health system was also presented as a part of a big business plan to rip off the population: RT's Lee Camp explained the long-term goal of the national health system to focus on treatment that brings money, rather than on pills that make people healthy (The World According to Jesse, 2020c).

RT's hosts were cherry picking stories that would help highlight the cynicism of the ruling elite. One of Ventura's shows discussed a possible military intervention in Yemen amidst the pandemic (The World According to Jesse, 2020e). Another discussed the media criticism of Tesla's founder Elon Musk for delivering a different kind of ventilator to California hospitals (Passantino, 2020). Ventura's response to the story boiled down to the traditional mantra of the big oil lobby in control of the media that used every opportunity to challenge Musk's electro cars. 'The oil business hates him' – concluded Ventura (The World According to Jesse, 2020f).

As opposed to broadcasts, the op-ed section became a source of unrestrained conspiratorial rhetoric and a showcase of RT's ability to attract diverse voices from all ideological walks (see, RT, 2020b). Analysis of the op-ed section demonstrates that it was incredibly welcoming for all sorts of COVID-dissidents, anti-vaxxers and government-critical extreme libertarians. For instance, Peter Andrews called for an end to the lockdown, on the grounds that the protocols for testing for coronavirus were flawed and meaningless. Although Andrews did not accuse anyone of being directly responsible for the mistakes in testing protocols and the political decisions made on their basis, he hinted at 'dark ruminations' generated by the fatal political and medical mistakes made during the pandemic (Andrews, 2020).

The op-ed section regularly raised concerns that the pandemic was a plot to suppress freedom of speech. Some argued that legitimate worries about the efficiency of anti-COVID measures were being portrayed as wacky conspiracy theories by scientists and the media, in ways reminiscent of communist-era psychological treatment of ideological opponents (Buyinski, 2020a). Some writers even urged politicians to listen to conspiracy theorists as they might vocalise some important issues that affect the societies where they arise (Wilson, 2020). At times, these radical expressions of conspiracy theories extended to the broadcast shows, but that was fairly rare. A London-based author, Lewis Olden, accused the UK government of running a cyber-censorship military operation that would ban alternative views and conspiracy theories about the lockdown rules:

> those who legitimately are sceptical about the circumstances in which a vaccine has been produced are being denied the right to voice their fears... they should always retain the right to speak their mind without fear of retribution, so long as they are not doing so in a threatening manner.
>
> (Olden, 2020)

The only conspiratorial allusion in which RT's content producers engaged openly is the notion of the COVID-pandemic as one of the ways to create world government, under the name 'the Great Reset'. RT's op-ed contributor Helen Buyinski described the New World Order-like plans of the World Economic Forum to introduce human screening and mandatory vaccinations as a form of control in the post-pandemic world (Buyinski, 2020b). Neil Clark (2020), a regular guest on RT shows, predicted a dystopian global order ruled by the billionaire who will abolish cash, restrict travel to those without vaccines and strip individuals of private property described in another piece as digital slavery. Another regular contributor, writer and technology consultant Norman Lewis (2020a), accused the global elite of creating conditions for the global pandemic and brainwashing progressive politicians to restructure their societies in the way the globalists wanted it. In order to visualise this global elite plot for the post-pandemic world, RT produced a striking three-minute video to illustrate how every aspect of human relations would be under the control of the financial and corporate elite (RT, 2020c).

The COVID global crisis proved to be an ideal opportunity to highlight Western governments' failures to provide fair treatment and support for ordinary people. The chaos unleashed by the rapid lockdowns and the panic caused by the disease provided a fruitful ground for all sorts of conspiratorial speculations. People's willingness to trade liberty for security became key to showing the beneficiaries (and possible authors) of the global pandemic – the state and security establishment. Yet, for the US context, the additional prospect of sharing conspiracy narratives was provided by the polarising US Presidential elections. 'If the globalists can convince healthy people to quarantine because they are somehow spreading infections they do not have, they can easily manipulate the entire election process using communist-inspired election software' – concluded RT's op-ed contributor Wayne Dupree (2020a).

Case 2: RT coverage of the US elections

The 2020 US Presidential elections were a major news story globally, producing near-saturation coverage across a wide range of international outlets. Our analysis over the month prior to and after the elections reveals that RT produced a continuum of critical content. At one end of the spectrum were in-depth analytical discussions of the pathologies of US democracy, which remained responsive to changing evidence, but were nonetheless situated within conspiratorial framings of US politics described above. At the other end of the spectrum were overt and evidence-free conspiracy theories about the election campaign and its core protagonists, which – as with the treatment of COVID-19 – tended to be concentrated in the op-ed section. Here, RT applied its blanket disclaimer of disassociation from the network. Such op-eds were aggressively promoted via RT's Facebook and Twitter accounts, whilst RT's Instagram feed took a mocking tone about both sides in the election. Overall, RT's social media channels 'foregrounded the narrative portraying a US democracy in disarray' (Tolz and Kazakov, 2020), and the general picture that emerged from election coverage across platforms and genres was one of a fundamentally flawed – not to mention corrupt – democratic system in the US.

Much of RT's analysis prior to the election outlined the pathologies of a dysfunctional political system (Watching the Hawks, 2020e).

Various programmes questioned whether this could be a 'Free and fair election?' given inadequate COVID provisions and an Electoral College system that distorts the people's will (The World According to Jesse, 2020g; Watching the Hawks, 2020f). Concerns about election meddling were presented as hypocritical given the state's alleged involvement as far afield as Bolivia and Ukraine (Watching the Hawks, 2020e).

The post-election period saw further focus on the pathologies of the US democratic system in which elites subvert the people's will: 'whereas the will of the people is expressed, it's the will of the few that is exercised' (Kazbek, 2020). In RT's accounts, systemic factors like gerrymandering and the Electoral College system 'make sure the American vote doesn't count the way it should' (Malagurski, 2020). Notably, this charge comes from an op-ed author described primarily as 'a Serbian Canadian documentary film director' – there is no mention that he fronted a short online video series for RT.[1]

Furthermore, despite the discussions of systemic problems prior to the election, many programmes disputed the post-election charges of the Trump administration, or claimed that any bias would actually benefit him. For example, after underlining that fraudulent ballots were highly unlikely to be successfully cast by mail, one guest noted 'a con job to knock out the ballots' in 2016 as evidence that mail-in voters could be illegally removed from election lists (The World According to Jesse, 2020h). As time passed and the Trump administration pursued its challenges to the election results, Jesse Ventura became more uncompromising: Trump was a 'little baby' whose claims looked 'utterly ridiculous', and he should stop his vexatious challenges, as they made 'people doubt our elections' (The World according to Jesse, 2020i).

Despite similar points being raised occasionally in the op-ed section, this heavily pro-Trump portion of RT's content was also a place where extreme conspiracy theories were articulated: Wayne Dupree regurgitated Trump campaign claims that 'with every passing day evidence of widespread fraud is mounting', and that the Democrats had delivered 'a rigged election' (Dupree, 2020b). The Presidential debates, for instance, were described as a 'chaotic car crash', in which 'two powerhouses of the two party corporate dictatorship' reproduced the kind of spin, non-answers and outright lies that people have come to expect from their political leaders (Watching the Hawks, 2020d, 2020h). The Commission for Presidential Debates was represented as a bipartisan scam intended to keep third-party candidates out, that only succeeds due to 'media complicity', as only 'acceptable' participants and questions are included (Watching the Hawks, 2020h). A key irony here is the extent to which RT itself relies upon a streamlined pool of repeat participants and partisan moderators in its own discussions.

One of the most important features of RT's discussion of such systemic inadequacies is the charge that they only remain possible due to the 'dirtbag hypocrites' of the political elites who choose not to fix bugs that 'they can get around it if they have to' when it favours them (The World According to Jesse, 2020j, CrossTalk, 2020c). In RT's accounts, both of the main political parties are implicated in this kind of hijacking of the democratic process, and the sentiment recurs in no uncertain terms throughout RT's op-eds, even those not about the election. There is the idea that those in 'the elite' or 'the Establishment' 'believe democracy has gone too far', and have 'little genuine love for democracy' when it brings to power those with populist views with which they do not sympathise (Furedi, 2020). For the most part, both candidates are represented as interchangeable defenders of a militaristic and persistent status quo, past their prime and driven by similar corporatist and fascistic tendencies, whose parties represent neither the interests of voters, nor the US as a whole (see Zizek, 2020a, 2020b; Buyinski, 2020c). Articles sympathetic to Trump paint him as the victim of an all-encompassing establishment resistance.

The Democratic Party is portrayed as being corrupt and dangerous (Chang, 2020). It is represented as a divided party with a victim culture that is 'complicit in rape.... [and] empowers perpetrators' (Reade, 2020). Leading Democrats are subject to character assassination, and many of RT's op-ed's cover conspiracy theories related to Hunter Biden and his business dealings, even repeating Trump's words in referring unironically (and without inverted commas) to 'the Biden crime family' (Fellerstein, 2020). As late as 9 November, op-eds were referring in delegitimising tones to the 'apparent victory' of Biden, as merely a return to the establishment's warmongering business as usual, the 'Great Reset' of global capitalism and the 'new pathologized totalitarianism' (Hopkins, 2020).

It is not just the two main parties that tend to be portrayed either as in league, or equivalent, within RT's coverage. Scientists are informed by 'a technocratic elitist view' (Lewis, 2020b); leaders of the Black community have traded 'their subservience to the white political leadership of the Democratic Party' for influence (Ritter, 2020a); Hollywood celebrities are part of a McCarthyite anti-Trump movement (Leeman, 2020) and the mainstream media and social media companies are simply 'establishment propagandists' (Buyinski, 2020d). Major tech giants are criticised for their 'outsized influence over commerce, speech, media and advertising' (The World According to Jesse,

2020g), including through their attempts to police the spread of conspiracy theories online. Such attempts are represented as an attack on free speech that suppresses genuine concerns about the electoral process, because the industry 'took Hillary Clinton's loss hard and wasn't going to let a rogue candidate win again' (Cox, 2020a). Despite some more analytically balanced outliers, the op-ed section tends to give such arguments a pro-Trump spin: allegations of pro-Democrat, anti-Trump bias abound, often coupled with the argument that this is essentially fear-mongering motivated by profit. The mainstream media is itself often accused of conspiracy theorising around the idea of potential Russian meddling in the election (CrossTalk, 2020d, 2020e). RT's Tweets dismissed reporters' allegations of election meddling[2] and mocked Clinton's renewed accusations of Russian meddling in the elections, which 'worked so well in 2016'.[3]

RT's coverage engaged in many instances not just with specific conspiracy theories, but also with the concept of conspiracy theories. These tended to be perceived in the activities of the mainstream media and political elites; or as a label that was an 'occupational hazard' for the critical thinker. In the former category lies the accusation that political elites rely on conspiracy theories to delegitimise their opponents – so that if Biden wins, Russiagate conspiracy theories will simply be replaced by Chinagate ones (Johnstone, 2020). In the latter category is an opening monologue from *CrossTalk*'s Lavelle, who declares that disagreeing with official narratives is what gains one the label of 'conspiracy theorist' despite what he presents as the fact that many official narratives are actually debunked conspiracy theories – particularly those relating to Putin and Russia (CrossTalk, 2020e, 2020f). Post-election programmes and op-eds similarly portrayed a range of issues – including 'Russiagate', climate change and suggestions that Trump would try to instigate a coup to stay in power, as establishment-backed conspiracy theories or hoaxes (Ritter, 2020b; CrossTalk, 2020g).

Nonetheless, RT's outputs did engage not just with a conspiratorial worldview, but also with the most extreme partisan conspiracy theories. Prior to the election itself, these tended to be focussed squarely within the op-ed section. Anti-Trump Republicans were deemed 'traitorous', whilst one writer referred to a proposed commission to govern the usurpation of Presidential powers as instituting 'a "Deep State"-like cabal, including former officials, to gate-keep the White House' (Malic, 2020a). What is more, on RT's news app, stories presenting relatively uncritical coverage of Trump's claims about the election dominated the feed, increasing the prevalence of allegations of fraud and electoral illegitimacy (Tolz and Kazakov, 2020). After the election, however, broadcast programmes increasingly engaged with conspiracy theories – though often dispelling those that came from the Trump camp. Thus, various immediate post-election programmes emphasised the lack of evidence of election manipulation on either side (Watching the Hawks, 2020g; The World According to Jesse, 2020k), and continued dispelling the Trump administration's allegations and conspiracy theories about the election as time progressed: 'If it was fixed for the democrats, why did the republicans do so well?' (The World According to Jesse, 2020l). Nonetheless, they retained a conspiratorial framing of US politics as a whole, as being dominated by corrupt parties in league with the defence and other industries, as well as the mainstream media.

CrossTalk significantly ramped up its explicit engagement with conspiracy theories following the elections. One episode was dedicated entirely to analysing the 'unaccountable deep state', which the presenter argued 'took capture of an entire administration and they are unapologetic about it'; his guest later asserted that 'Joe Biden is one of 'em'. This episode had already been viewed over 10,600 times in the first two weeks after its upload to YouTube (CrossTalk, 2020h). A subsequent episode interrogated the idea of the Great Reset, with Lavelle and guests agreeing that the Trump administration represented the biggest break in a cycle of foreign policy continuity between Presidential administrations (CrossTalk, 2020g).

Again, however, it was in the op-ed section that such conspiracy theories were expressed at their most extreme, with repeated references made to the nefarious activities of the 'deep state'. Intelligence officials' joint statement asserting that the Kremlin was behind the Hunter Biden story was portrayed as an example of when 'the Deep State provided cover' (Cox, 2020a). Despite Trump's best efforts, his Presidency ultimately confirmed that it is 'entrenched political interests that really run Washington' (Buyinski, 2020e). Ultimately, the Biden victory is presented not just as a return to business as usual, but as a victory for the entrenched interests of 'the big capital and deep state apparatus, from Google and Microsoft to the FBI and the National Security Agency' (Zizek, 2020b).

Global shocks and business as usual

RT's reporting of the COVID-19 pandemic and the 2020 US Presidential election campaign show how adept the network has become at applying the core features of its approach to newsmaking – and the integration of conspiracy theories within that – to both unanticipated and entirely predictable political crises. As discussed in relation to the

Skripal case in Chapter 5, RT's reliance on counter-mainstream perspectives and voices from the margins gives it a peculiar advantage in reporting stories defined by a lack of concrete information. This same tendency was evident in its reporting of COVID-19. At every stage of the story's development, RT foregrounded questions and speculation, whilst slotting these neatly within RT's preferred world view of a fundamentally corrupt environment of media, political and corporate collaborations. Where opportunities arose to make allegations of institutional Russophobia – as with the criticisms of the Sputnik vaccine approval process – RT enthusiastically took these up, insinuating that criticisms were nothing more than Western institutions' Russophobic reactions to a medical success. This reliance on standard conspiratorial tropes was even more evident in RT's coverage of the 2020 election campaign. Whilst broadcast coverage tended to restrict its conspiratorial allegations to the nature of the system and the fundamentally flawed democratic process in the US, RT's op-ed section platformed all manner of extreme and explicit conspiracy theories about the process, the parties and the individuals involved in the election. Once again, this did not involve the production of outrageous claims by RT itself: the network effectively capitalised on the rich seam of partisan conspiracy theorising around the elections, and slotted these within its broader preferred editorial line of systemic failure and corruption. The network's engagements with these claims and commentators mirrored the patterns of their broader interactions online. As our concluding chapter demonstrates, this speaks to the effectiveness with which RT has evolved over the course of its existence to best fit its operations to the realities of the overarching political and media environment.

Notes

1 Playlist available here: https://www.youtube.com/playlist?list=PLBRLK mBip431UBIYPE0vj8NwDLXrji4ML
2 @RT_com, August 10th, 2020, available at: https://twitter.com/RT_com/ status/1292717315415515136
3 @RT_com, February 21st, 2020, available at: https://twitter.com/RT_com/ status/1230962417200435200

References

Andrews, P. (2020). 'A Global Team of Experts Has Found 10 FATAL FLAWS in the Main Test for Covid and Is Demanding It's Urgently Axed. As They Should', *RT*, 1 December [Online]. Available at: https://www.rt.com/ op-ed/508383-fatal-flaws-covid-test/ (Accessed: 16 December 2020).

BBC News. (2020). 'Coronavirus: Putin Says Vaccine Has Been Approved for Use', 11 August [Online]. Available at: https://www.bbc.co.uk/news/world-europe-53735718 (Accessed: 16 December 2020).

Buyinski, H. (2020a). "Conspiracy Theories' on Covid-19 Come from BRAIN DAMAGE? Questionable Science Is Being Used to Pathologize Real Dissent', *RT*, 19 November [Online]. Available at: https://www.rt.com/op-ed/507210-unscientific-paper-pathologize-dissent-miller/ (Accessed: 16 December 2020).

Buyinski, H. (2020b). "Health Passports' for Air Travel Mean Mandatory Covid-19 Vaccines Cloaked in the Illusion of Choice', *RT*, 24 November [Online]. Available at: https://www.rt.com/op-ed/507706-iata-vaccine-passport-mandate/ (Accessed: 16 December 2020).

Buyinski, H. (2020c). 'Black Panderers: Trump & Biden's Fight for African American Vote Is a Grotesque Pantomime of Caring', *RT*, 16 October [Online]. Available at: https://www.rt.com/op-ed/503690-trump-biden-african-american-vote/ (Accessed: 16 December 2020).

Buyinski, H. (2020d). 'Gloating Neocons Proposing Ideological Genocide Hint at What's Really on the Menu When Biden 'Builds Back Better'', *RT*, 9 November [Online]. Available at: https://www.rt.com/op-ed/506230-trump-accountability-attack-dissent-neoliberals/ (Accessed: 16 December 2020).

Buyinski, H. (2020e). 'Trump's Reign Has Proved the US President Is Merely a Figurehead. Does It Really Matter Who Wins the Vote?', *RT*, 5 November [Online]. Available at: https://www.rt.com/op-ed/505758-trump-us-president-win-vote/ (Accessed: 16 December 2020).

Chang, C. (2020). 'Reaction to Biden's 'Win' Shows That Leftists Will Never Be Happy, Because They Always Want to Play the Victim', *RT*, 22 November [Online]. Available at: https://www.rt.com/op-ed/507297-biden-win-leftists-play-victim/ (Accessed: 16 December 2020).

Clark, N. (2020). 'If the 'Great Reset' Really Is So Good for Us, Let's Hold a Referendum on It, So It Can Have a Democratic Mandate (or Not)'. Available at: https://www.rt.com/op-ed/507336-great-reset-world-economic-forum/ (Accessed: 16 December 2020).

Cox, T. (2020a). 'Under Biden, Big Tech's Censorship Goons Will Make Conservatives Nostalgic for the Days of Relatively Free Speech in Obama Era', *RT*, 9 November [Online]. Available at: https://www.rt.com/op-ed/506204-biden-big-tech-censorship/ (Accessed: 16 December 2020).

CrossTalk. (2020a). 'Coronavirus Fears', *RT*, 4 March [Online]. Available at: https://www.rt.com/shows/crosstalk/482232-coronavirus-global-health-danger/ (Accessed: 16 December 2020).

CrossTalk. (2020b). 'CrossTalk Bullhorns: Covid-19', *RT*, 16 March [Online]. Available at: https://www.rt.com/shows/crosstalk/483150-covid-19-pandemic-globalization/ (Accessed: 16 December 2020).

CrossTalk. (2020c). 'Free and Fair?', *RT*, 11 November [Online]. Available at: https://www.rt.com/shows/crosstalk/506266-stolen-us-presidential-election/ (Accessed: 16 December 2020).

CrossTalk. (2020d). 'Media in Denial', *RT*, 28 October [Online]. Available at: https://www.rt.com/shows/crosstalk/504663-media-control-speech-freedom/ (Accessed: 16 December 2020).

CrossTalk. (2020e). 'Russia! Russia! Russia!', *RT*, 30 October [Online]. Available at: https://www.rt.com/shows/crosstalk/504900-russia-conspiracy-political-discourse/ (Accessed: 16 December 2020).

CrossTalk. (2020f). 'Whose Conspiracy?', *RT*, 19 October [Online]. Available at: https://www.rt.com/shows/crosstalk/503833-conspiracy-theories-narrative-populism/ (Accessed: 16 December 2020).

CrossTalk. (2020g). 'Build Back Worse?', *RT*, 31 October [Online]. Available at: https://www.rt.com/shows/crosstalk/508161-biden-administration-foreign-policy/ (Accessed: 16 December 2020).

CrossTalk. (2020h). 'Unaccountable Deep State', *RT*, 27November. [Online]. Available at: https://www.rt.com/shows/crosstalk/507870-russiagate-hoax-biden-administration/ (Accessed: 16 December 2020).

Dupree, W. (2020a). 'Wayne Dupree: My family Thanksgiving this Week Will Be Business as Usual. There'll Be No Covid Restrictions at My Dinner Table', *RT*, 23 November [Online]. Available at: https://www.rt.com/op-ed/507563-wayne-dupree-thanksgiving-covid/ (Accessed: 16 December 2020).

Dupree, W. (2020b).'Wayne Dupree: Trump Isn't Going Anywhere and Shouldn't. With a Brilliant Lawyer like Sidney Powell on His Side, He's Going to Win!', *RT*, 16 November [Online]. Available at: https://www.rt.com/op-ed/506865-wayne-dupree-trump-lawyer/ (Accessed: 16 December 2020).

Fellerstein, M. (2020). ''He's Back': The Last Week Has Illustrated the MSM and Establishment Bias against Trump, but Despite That He'll Still Win Election', *RT*, 16 October [Online]. Available at: https://www.rt.com/op-ed/502661-msm-establishment-trump-win/ (Accessed: 16 December 2020).

Ferrada de Noli, M. (2020). 'I'm an Epidemiology Professor and I Have Some Genuine Concerns about the AstraZeneca Covid Vaccine. Here's Why...', *RT*, 26 November [Online]. Available at: https://www.rt.com/op-ed/507931-covid-19-astrazeneca-vaccine-concerns/ (Accessed: 16 December 2020).

Frawley, A. (2020). 'Docs for Sale: US Government Issues Rare Fraud Alert as Big Pharma Spends Billions Bribing Medics to Prescribe Their Drugs', *RT*, 20 November [Online]. Available at: https://www.rt.com/op-ed/507355-big-pharma-dhs-fraud/ (Accessed: 16 December 2020).

Furedi, F. (2020). 'The Elite Say Too Much Democracy Is Undemocratic, But They Just Want to Stop the 'Wrong Sort of People' Winning Elections', *RT*, 7 October [Online]. Available at: https://www.rt.com/op-ed/502839-elite-too-much-democracy/ (Accessed: 16 December 2020).

Hopkins, C.J. (2020). 'The War Is Over ... Global Capitalism Triumphs!', *RT*, 10 November [Online]. Available at: https://www.rt.com/op-ed/506307-war-over-globocap-triumphs/ (Accessed: 16 December 2020).

Johnstone, C. (2020). 'Caitlin Johnstone: If Biden Wins, Russiagate Will Magically Morph into Chinagate', *RT*, 31 October [Online]. Available at: https://www.rt.com/op-ed/505077-trump-russiagate-biden-chinagate/ (Accessed: 16 December 2020).

Kazbek, K. (2020). 'When the Choice Is between Trump and Biden, American Elections Don't Seem That Democratic', *RT*, 10 October [Online]. Available at: https://www.rt.com/op-ed/502851-trump-biden-us-democracy/ (Accessed: 16 December 2020).

Leeman, Z. (2020). 'Democrats Are Giving McCarthyism a Major Comeback with Blacklists for Trump Supporters, and We Should All Be Worried', *RT*, 11 November [Online]. Available at: https://www.rt.com/op-ed/506426-trump-supporters-blacklist-mccarthy/ (Accessed: 16 December 2020).

Lewis, N. (2020a). 'An Elite-led 'Great Reset' post-Covid? No, What We Need First Is to Get Rid of the Globalist Approach That Got Us into This Mess', *RT*, 18 November. [Online]. Available at: https://www.rt.com/op-ed/507108-great-reset-wef-globalist/ (Accessed: 16 December 2020).

Lewis, N. (2020b). 'The Death Knell of Science Is Being Sounded, Not by Politicians but by Partisan Scientists Themselves', *RT*, 8 October [Online]. Available at: https://www.rt.com/op-ed/502948-death-knell-science-politics/ (Accessed: 16 December 2020).

Malagurski, B. (2020). 'True Democracy Was Never among the Founding Principles of the US, Why Should Anyone Be Surprised by the Election Chaos?', *RT*, 12 November [Online]. Available at: https://www.rt.com/op-ed/506515-democracy-founding-principles-us/ (Accessed: 16 December 2020).

Malic, N. (2020a). '"Deep State' Much? Pelosi and Raskin's 25th Amendment Body Would Let Unelected Bureaucrats Override the Will of American People', *RT*, 9 October. Available at: https://www.rt.com/op-ed/503097-pelosi-25a-commission-deep-state/ (Accessed: 16 December 2020).

Olden, L. (2020). 'UK Wants to Use Literal Army to Fight 'anti-Vaccine Propaganda' Online. Are We in a Budding Totalitarian State?', *RT*, 2 December [Online]. Available at: https://www.rt.com/op-ed/508478-uk-anti-vaccine-propaganda/ (Accessed: 16 December 2020).

Passantino, J. (2020). 'Elon Musk Says He Sent Ventilators to California Hospitals, They Say They Got Something Else Instead', *CNN*, 17 April [Online]. Available at: https://edition.cnn.com/2020/04/17/tech/elon-musk-ventilators-california/index.html (Accessed: 16 December 2020).

Reade, T. (2020). 'Tara Reade & Rose McGowan: Surviving Rape Culture and the Democratic Cult', *RT*, 1 December [Online]. Available at: https://www.rt.com/op-ed/508306-tara-reade-rose-mcgowan-rape-culture/ (Accessed: 16 December 2020).

Ritter, S. (2020a). 'Maga Was Far More Mainstream than Most Americans Realized, and Its Electoral Rejection Will Prove to Be a Historic Mistake', *RT*, 10 November [Online]. Available at: https://www.rt.com/

op-ed/506279-maga-mainstream-donald-trump/ (Accessed: 16 December 2020).

Ritter, S. (2020b). 'No, Trump's Firing of Defense Secretary Mark Esper Doesn't Mean There's Going to Be a Military Coup in the US', *RT*, 10 November [Online]. Available at: https://www.rt.com/op-ed/506319-us-trump-defense-secretary-sacking-coup/ (Accessed: 16 December 2020).

RT. (2020a). 'Why Isn't COVID-19 Spreading as Rapidly in Russia?', 23 March [Online]. Available at: https://youtu.be/tDeYOzJJk_Y (Accessed: 16 December 2020).

RT. (2020b). 'UK Terrorism Chief Calls for 'National Debate' on Criminalizing Doubts about Covid-19 Vaccine', *RT*, 24 November [Online]. Available at: https://www.rt.com/uk/507207-vaccine-hesitancy-terrorism-question-basu/ (Accessed: 16 December 2020).

RT. (2020c). 'The Great Reset', *RT*, 15 October [Online]. Available at: https://youtu.be/_wm5NrlpaCQ (Accessed: 16 December 2020).

RT. (2020d). 'A Deadly Cocktail: Spies, Cell Phone Records and the Poisoned Negroni Behind Bellingcat's Navalny 'Expose'', *RT*, 15 December [Online]. Available at: https://www.rt.com/russia/509757-navalny-poisoning-bellingcat-expose/ (Accessed: 16 December 2020).

The World According to Jesse. (2020a). 'Jimmy Dore & Rick Sanchez Destroy MSM's New Red-baiting Campaign', *RT*, 29 February [Online]. Available at: https://www.rt.com/shows/the-world-according-to-jesse/481876-msm-russian-thread-us-politics/ (Accessed: 16 December 2020).

The World According to Jesse. (2020b). 'Jimmy Dore: 'You're Only as Healthy as the Least Insured Person around You'', *RT*, 7 March [Online]. Available at: https://www.rt.com/shows/the-world-according-to-jesse/482460-who-coronavirus-outbreak-statement/ (Accessed: 16 December 2020).

The World According to Jesse. (2020c). 'Lee Camp Sounds Off on Coronavirus Epidemic and Chelsea Manning's Release', *RT*, 21 March [Online]. Available at: https://www.rt.com/shows/the-world-according-to-jesse/483659-coronavirus-outbreak-stock-market-trump/ (Accessed: 16 December 2020).

The World According to Jesse. (2020d). 'Netanyahu on Trial', *RT*, 30 May [Online]. Available at: https://www.rt.com/shows/the-world-according-to-jesse/490142-netanyahu-trial-covid19-deregulations/ (Accessed: 16 December 2020).

The World According to Jesse. (2020e). 'Jesse Ventura: We Should Be Fighting against a Virus, Not Waging War in Yemen', *RT*, 18 April [Online]. Available at: https://www.rt.com/shows/the-world-according-to-jesse/486078-saudi-arabia-war-end-yemen/ (Accessed: 16 December 2020).

The World According to Jesse. (2020f). 'Jesse Ventura: 'Oil-funded MSM Attacks Tesla's Elon Musk for Coronavirus Response', *RT*, 25 April [Online]. Available at: https://www.rt.com/shows/the-world-according-to-jesse/486730-musk-medical-equipment-california/ (Accessed: 16 December 2020).

The World According to Jesse. (2020g). 'The Dirt on Clean Energy', *RT*, 25 October [Online]. Available at: https://www.rt.com/shows/the-world-according-to-jesse/504449-clean-energy-ecology-price/ (Accessed: 16 December 2020).

The World According to Jesse. (2020h). 'Stimulus Halt Leave Millions Broke', *RT*, 10 October [Online]. Available at: https://www.rt.com/shows/the-world-according-to-jesse/503045-stimulus-halt-millions-broke/ (Accessed: 16 December 2020).

The World According to Jesse. (2020i). 'Election Denialism Plagues US', *RT*, 14 November [Online]. Available at: https://www.rt.com/shows/the-world-according-to-jesse/506634-election-denialism-meth-epidemic/ (Accessed: 16 December 2020).

The World According to Jesse. (2020j). 'China Sanctions US Firms for Taiwan Arms Sale', *RT*, 31 October [Online]. Available at: https://www.rt.com/shows/the-world-according-to-jesse/504999-judge-confirmation-arms-sale-discovery/ (Accessed: 16 December 2020).

The World According to Jesse. (2020k). 'Journalists Call Out Media Censorship', *RT*, 7 November [Online]. Available at: https://www.rt.com/shows/the-world-according-to-jesse/505969-media-censorship-voter-suppression/ (Accessed: 16 December 2020).

The World According to Jesse. (2020l). 'The Coming of a Vaccine', *RT*, 24 November [Online]. Available at: https://www.rt.com/shows/the-world-according-to-jesse/508024-vaccine-technology-covid19-economy/ (Accessed: 16 December 2020).

Tolz, V. and Hutchings, S. (2020). 'COVID-19 Disinformation: Two Short Reports on the Russian Dimension', 6 April [Online]. Available at: https://reframingrussia.com/2020/04/06/covid-19-disinformation-two-short-reports-on-the-russian-dimension/ (Accessed: 16 December 2020).

Tolz, V. and Kazakov, V. (2020). 'The US Presidential Election through a Russian Media Lens: From Domestic Legitimacy to Global (Mis)Information', 24 November [Online]. Available at: https://reframingrussia.com/2020/11/24/the-us-presidential-election-through-a-russian-media-lens-from-domestic-legitimacy-to-global-misinformation/ (Accessed: 16 December 2020).

Watching the Hawks. (2020a). 'A Coronavirus Patriot Act & The Economics of a Pandemic', *RT*, 24 March [Online]. Available at: https://www.rt.com/shows/watching-the-hawks/483910-dan-kovalik-no-more-war-book/ (Accessed: 16 December 2020).

Watching the Hawks. (2020b). 'Protesting against #Covid19 Lockdowns & Police Repression during the Crisis', *RT*, 21 April [Online]. Available at: https://www.rt.com/shows/watching-the-hawks/486394-coronavirus-lockdown-rallies-usa/ (Accessed: 16 December 2020).

Watching the Hawks. (2020c). 'US Response: Profits over People & Congress' So-called Stimulus Package', *RT*, 25 March. [Online]. Available at: https://www.rt.com/shows/watching-the-hawks/484015-coronavirus-stimulus-package-congress-negotiations/ (Accessed: 16 December 2020).

Watching the Hawks. (2020d). 'Presidential Debates, Education Bribery, and Halloween Frights!', *RT*, 24 October [Online]. Available at: https://www.rt.com/shows/watching-the-hawks/504445-presidential-debates-biden-race/ (Accessed: 16 December 2020).

Watching the Hawks. (2020e). 'Election to Cost $14 billion, While US Points Finger at Foreign Elections', *RT*, 7 November [Online]. Available at: https://www.rt.com/shows/watching-the-hawks/505972-counting-votes-foreign-elections/ (Accessed: 16 December 2020).

Watching the Hawks. (2020f). 'US Workers Appeal to UN for Help', *RT*, 9 October [Online]. Available at: https://www.rt.com/shows/watching-the-hawks/502911-us-firms-labor-law-violation/ (Accessed: 16 December 2020).

Watching the Hawks. (2020g). 'Jesse Ventura, John Kiriakou Discuss Elections, Drugs, and Third Parties', *RT*, 5 November [Online]. Available at: https://www.rt.com/shows/watching-the-hawks/505667-john-kiriakou-presidential-elections/ (Accessed: 16 December 2020).

Watching the Hawks. (2020h). 'Presidential Debates or Presidential Advertising?', *RT*, 10 October [Online]. Available at: https://www.rt.com/shows/watching-the-hawks/503037-presidential-debates-advertising-big-tech/ (Accessed: 16 December 2020).

Watching the Hawks. (2020i). 'An Inauguration of Legal Bribery & The Big Business of Fake People', *RT*, 3 December [Online]. Available at: https://www.rt.com/shows/watching-the-hawks/508517-biden-presidential-inauguration-bribery/ (Accessed: 16 December 2020).

Wilson, D. (2020). 'As the German Lockdown Movement Continues to Grow, Wild Claims of Nazi-era Laws and Anne Frank Comparisons Undermine Its Efforts', *RT*, 18 November. [Online]. Available at: https://www.rt.com/op-ed/507126-germany-qanon-covid-conspiracy/ (Accessed: 16 December 2020).

Zizek, S. (2020a). 'Slavoj Zizek: Biden's Just Trump with a Human Face, and the Two of Them Share the Same Enemy', *RT*, 27 October [Online]. Available at: https://www.rt.com/op-ed/504705-slavoj-zizek-biden-trump/ (Accessed: 16 December 2020).

Zizek, S. (2020b). 'Slavoj Zizek: Biden's Win Changes Nothing and Signifies Stalemate That Could See Trump Run Again in 2024', *RT*, 9 November [Online]. Available at: https://www.rt.com/op-ed/506197-zizek-biden-win-changes-nothing/ (Accessed: 16 December 2020).

Conclusion

In the 15 years of its existence, RT has learnt how to creatively deal with conspiracy theories to rhetorically undermine the positions of the Kremlin's opponents. The two main milestones important for RT's evolution discussed in this book – the war in Georgia in 2008 and the Crimea annexation in 2014 – helped the network to fine tune its approach not only to conspiracy theories but also to coverage of European and American politics, as well as to projecting Russia's role in the world.

As we are writing these lines, the Kremlin is facing the fallout of yet another massive political challenge in which politics, evidence, conspiracy and representation collide: *Bellingcat* in collaboration with *CNN, The Insider* and *Der Spiegel* released an investigation into how the Kremlin approved the poisoning of Russia's lead oppositional politician, Alexei Navalny in August 2020. Investigators obtained leaked GPS data from within Russia's corrupt law enforcement system, showing the FSB following and poisoning Navalny (Lister et al., 2020). The shock of the investigation was so big that the Kremlin kept silence for three days (Putin's spokesperson Dmitry Peskov even cancelled a daily presser). RT was one of the few state outlets to offer prompt coverage of the story, reporting some of *Bellingcat*'s key allegations which none of the domestic Russian media dared to report.

What is notable in RT's report is the way in which it uses the presented facts to distort and undermine the findings of 'the mainstream media' that threaten the Kremlin's image. First, the article makes humorous dismissals of the story, so that both the crime and human tragedy seem less serious (i.e. calling it a 'novichoktail'). Second, the piece highlights potential inconsistencies in the story and reiterates its frequent disparagement of *Bellingcat* for possible connections with intelligence agencies, as well as unclear sources of funding. It asks whether the findings of *Bellingcat* can be trusted given concerns regarding the outfit's professionalism: are they amateurs or are they professionals? Third, true to form, it ignores other collaborators – like the investigative reporters of *The Insider* – that aren't so easily disparaged. Finally, the report uses historical examples as evidence for why intelligence agencies' pronouncements on this case cannot be trusted. All of these clues and conspiratorial allegations are made to provide RT's hosts and guests with a pre-curated menu of dismissals, as well as to muddy the waters in the search for the real beneficiaries of Navalny's poisoning. Whether this tactic is effective for foreign audiences or not is a question that is not easy to answer, but RT's traditional agenda and the major international crises of the decade have prepared it well to set up its coverage of even such a controversial – and potentially damaging – news item. RT's rather scant reporting on Navalny after his return to Russia and subsequent arrest has repurposed such dismissals and disparagement.

RT has long positioned itself within the comfortable niche of the underdog-truthteller that can take on any government, media outlet or transnational corporation. The first thing that an attentive viewer pays attention to watching RT's broadcasts is a recurrence of populist utterances: big business, corrupt government, the imperialism and military expansion of the US, and the lavish lifestyles of American elites on both sides of the political divide. These topics are so regularly pushed by RT that some seasons of shows effectively merge into one super long episode. By posing as an alternative to 'mainstream media', RT not only brands itself to attract potential viewers and followers of such content, it also seeks to show that the traditional media is dead and the road is open for all sorts of non-conventional approaches to news and current affairs.

RT co-opts issues from both the right and the left side of the political spectrum, giving the network a unique opportunity to platform all sorts of guests: from no name bloggers/freelance journalists to mainstream politicians or reputable presenters. RT's programmes very often rely on the same set of speakers, a notable proportion of whom are directly affiliated either with the channel, or its sister outlet, Sputnik. Their role as guests is not just to share an (often predictable) point of view: they also serve to vocalise the most extreme points, offering the network a level of plausible distance from those points and an aura of journalistic integrity. It is worth pointing out that RT's dispassionate contributors are very clear that their interests are in bringing a diversity of points to RT's audience. Nevertheless, our analysis shows that RT pre-curates the perspectives that it includes within its coverage of key issues and will continue to do so. Not only is this a pragmatic approach in a political and media environment in which RT is viewed with suspicion by many who might otherwise have served as guests, but also the reliance on 'network friends' gives some baseline predictability as to how they will comment on even unanticipated future crises and events.

It is very easy to caricature RT as merely a 'Russian propaganda' brand – as many have done in the aftermath of the Crimean annexation and successive Russian meddling scandals. But in fact, RT is a product of, and a savvy player in, a broader global media environment. This context for RT's evolution is vital as in today's world communication is not a one-way process. On the contrary, news coverage is a product of the interactions of journalists, host platforms and audiences with that content. All of these elements contribute to the ways in which populist messages are constructed and developed. Together, they work to give conspiratorial online content a comparative circulatory advantage. Positioning itself as an outside voice, RT chose conspiracy theories as its key content. They have become, in a way, a part of RT's identity.

What is important to note is that RT's staff seems to take on board the idea of conspiracy theories as a peculiar way to discuss the complicated reality around us. They realise the potential of conspiracy theories both to enlighten audiences about the genuine injustices of existing societal institutions, and to undermine the legitimacy of political actors. RT's presenters, who have less freedom to speculate without providing evidence, regularly opt for the principle: 'You can call me a conspiracy theorist, but I do my own research and just ask questions!' that relieves them from responsibility and opens up to further guesswork from reliable guests and op-ed contributors. RT provides the floor for those who spread conspiracy theories – claiming to be champions in the freedom of speech. However, across the range of RT's news stories, videos and op-eds posted online, these are expressed along a continuum of conspiracy. This ranges from pseudo-rational logics intended to appeal to self-styled critical thinkers, all the way through to the wildest of speculations that fit within RT's anti-elite/anti-Western agenda.

Our analysis highlights how RT has accomplished an evolutionary process of engaging with conspiracy theories that now helps the channel to engage very creatively with that type of content. The launch of RT America in 2010 demonstrated just how well some of RT's conspiratorial programmes and web articles play in the US market. The Crimean watershed as well as Ofcom's investigations in the UK has laid bare for RT just how fine the line is between marketable engagement with conspiracy theories, and reputational damage. RT's evolution has led to a situation in which, on the one hand, news that does not directly affect Russian interests is carefully reported (though according to RT's preferred framing and reporting values), whilst conspiracy theories stand as a crucial element of that reporting outsourced to guests or op-ed authors. On the other hand, once Russia's interests are involved, RT can engage fiercely in the battle with the 'mainstream media' using conspiracy theories as a primary tool for delegitimising opponents, whilst spotting 'Russophobia' – anti-Russian plots – everywhere. The involvement of loyal speakers and even high-ranking politicians is a central part of this process.

On the practical side, RT's evolution as both product and navigator of the contemporary media system has a fundamental impact on how we can go about addressing the phenomenon. First, the relative success of Ofcom in the UK and the Macron administration in France at curbing the worst excesses in RT's coverage both suggest that comprehensive media oversight is relatively effective at stemming the flow of outright media falsehoods – certainly when it comes to traditional platform output. Such regulation, however, must encompass statutory duties of broadcast media and social media platforms, a clarification of the responsibilities of content producers versus hosts, and cross-sector collaboration, plus transnational intergovernmental coordination of penalties for non-compliance. The market incentives for clickable content mean that policy responses must be addressed towards the whole (multiplatform) environment, rather than focussed on one actor within it. What is crucial here is that regulation is consistently applied, and RT is treated no differently than other outlets: this simply supports their own brand identity, feeds their conspiratorial narratives about threats to freedom of speech, and brings their content to the attention of those least likely to assess it critically.

Second, more complex in the case of RT is how conspiracy theories allow audiences to connect their own dots, whilst the network walks the tightrope of defensible journalistic practice. In fact, RT is just one of many alternative media outlets that positions itself as a free-thinker's best friend, presenting conspiracy theories as pseudo-logical arguments. Since experimental research has shown that these kinds of arguments tend to resonate most with those who consistently overestimate their critical thinking abilities (Douglas et al., 2017), comprehensive media literacy education is indispensable to disrupt this tactic both for RT and other fringe media (COMPACT, 2020). However, given the prevalence of conspiracy theorising amongst middle-aged and older demographic groups, education must reach beyond young digital natives. Such programmes need to be supported by adequate investment, which could derive in part from a social media levy. Crucially, though, any initiatives focussed on improved media literacy and critical thinking skills cannot be used to shift the responsibility for confronting conspiratorial media practices onto individuals. As our analysis has consistently shown, the propagation of conspiracy theories in today's integrated media environment is facilitated by the nature of that environment itself. Any effective solution must begin with genuinely systemic interventions.

Third, RT's engagement with conspiracy theories is contingent on their pre-existing popularity in the societies in which it operates. This, in turn, is related to longer term trends of decreasing trust in established political and media institutions, which are by no means easy to reverse. What is clear is that inconsistencies and hypocrisies around established social norms are conducive to the spread of conspiracy theories, especially when infringements are committed by political elites and within established institutions. Political actors must avoid undermining democracy's core values for short-term political gains. To make sure that such a commitment is not entirely contingent on political convention or will, transparent institutional safeguards are vital. In effect this means better holding politicians to account for their words and actions at the professional, rather than purely social, level – with binding codes of conduct and clear and consistent penalties for breaching them.

Events of 2020 have demonstrated not only that conspiracy theories are likely to remain an important part of the current political and media environment, but also that they can arise seemingly out of nowhere, and that they take on a particular potency at times of political crisis. RT, for its part, has perfectly evolved to capitalise on such instances of political crisis, when levels of verified information are low or in flux, and levels of institutional mistrust are high. Yet, it is not the network itself that is the source of many of these conspiracy theories, nor the underlying social schisms that cause their resonance. It functions as part of a broader political and media environment. Conspiracy theories will likely continue playing an important role in this context, so it is vital to set aside reactionary responses to RT and outlets like it, and instead focus on long-term, rational steps that will ensure both the integrity and transparency of political and media institutions, citizens' capacity to productively engage with them, and the comprehensive systemic safeguards necessary to keep these factors in balance.

References

COMPACT. (2020). 'Guide to Conspiracy Theories', *COMPACT Education Group*. Available at: https://ec.europa.eu/info/live-work-travel-eu/coronavirus-response/fighting-disinformation/identifying-conspiracy-theories_en (Accessed: 16 December 2020).

Douglas, K., Sutton, R.M., and Chichoka, A. (2017). 'The Psychology of Conspiracy Theories', *Current Directions in Psychological Science*, 26(6), 538–542.

Lister, T., Ward, C., and Shukla, S. (2020). 'CNN-Bellingcat Investigation Identifies Russian Specialists Who Trailed Putin's Nemesis Alexey Navalny before He Was Poisoned', *CNN*, 15 December [Online]. Available at: https://edition.cnn.com/2020/12/14/europe/russia-navalny-agents-bellingcat-ward/index.html (Accessed: 16 December 2020).

Index

9/11 34–35, 37
2018 World Cup 76

Adekvatnost 23–24
anti-Semitism 7
APN (News agency) 22

Babich, Dmitry 54–55, 60
BBC 12, 14, 23, 33
Bellingcat 71, 75, 101
Biden, Joseph 91–93
Bin Laden, Osama 37
Black Lives Matter 47
Bloomberg, Michael 42
Bolsheviks, The 21
bots 47, 54

Chepiga, Anatoly 71, 75
CIA 39, 45, 47, 53, 55–57, 59
Clinton, Hillary 39, 53, 57,
    59–61, 92
COINTELPRO 47
Corbyn, Jeremy 27–28
COVID–19 pandemic 63,
    85–89
CrossTalk 54–55, 59–61, 78, 85–86,
    92–93

deep state 46, 57–59, 92–93
DNC 53, 56, 59–62
Dupree, Wayne 89–90

Facebook 6–7, 10, 12, 48, 89
fake news 10, 12–13
false flag operation 44, 73
FBI 47, 53, 56, 93

Galloway, George 34, 76
Great Reset 88
Gromov, Aleksei 24

Illuminati, The 1
Iraq 34–35, 37, 45
ISIS 55

JFK 46
Jones, Alex 39

Kiselev, Dmitry 24

Lavelle, Peter 54–55, 86, 92–93
Lavrov, Sergey 70, 73
Lesin, Mikhail 25

Maddow, Rachel 37
May, Theresa 69–70
McCarthyism 7, 57, 91
media regulation 76, 104
Mironyuk, Svetlana 23–26
Mishkin, Alexander 71, 75
Monsanto 40
Mueller, Robert 53, 56, 61
Murdock, Rupert 42–43
Musk, Elon 87

NATO 45, 75
Navalny, Alexei 101–102
'New world order' 21, 38, 40, 41, 88
Novichok 70, 73, 78

Obama, Barack 38, 56, 58
Ofcom 33, 73, 78, 103
Orange revolution in Ukraine 20

Pavlovsky, Gleb 20–21, 23
Pizzagate 10
Pence, Mike 61
populism 9–11, 20, 102–103
Porton Down 74–75
propaganda 2, 7, 21, 25, 28–29, 56, 75, 103
Protocols of the Elders of Zion, The 7
Putin, Vladimir 19–21, 26, 53, 58, 70

QAnon 11

RIA Novosti 23
Rockefellers, The 41
Rothschilds 41
Russia report 78
Russophobia 57, 62, 74, 76, 94, 104
Russiagate 92

Salmond, Alex 34
Simonyan, Margarita 24–26, 28, 71
Sochi Olympic Games 25, 43
Soros, George 13

Sovinformbiuro (Soviet information bureau) 21–22
Sputnik (media) 13, 54, 62, 76–77, 102
Surkov, Vladislav 20
Syria 28, 33–34, 39, 45
Skripals, The 28, 63, 69–71, 76

trolls 54
Trump, Donald 34, 53, 58, 93
Truthers, The 36
Twitter 55, 61

U.F.O. 46

Ventura, Jesse 34, 45, 86–87
Ventura, Tyrell 54, 86

Wall street 40, 41
Washington, George 36
WikiLeaks 53–54, 59

Yanukovich, Viktor 45
Youtube 71

Zakharova, Maria 73